BRICKWORK
FOR THE GARDEN

BRICKWORK
FOR THE GARDEN
Including 16 easy-to-build projects

A L A N   &   G I L L   B R I D G E W A T E R

Published by Silverdale Books
an imprint of Bookmart Ltd in 2005

Bookmart Ltd
Blaby Road, Wigston
Leicester LE18 4SE

Registered Number 2372865

ISBN 1 84509 354 2

Editorial Direction: Rosemary Wilkinson
Senior Editor: Clare Sayer
Production: Hazel Kirkman

Designed and created for New Holland by AG&G BOOKS
Designer: Glyn Bridgewater
Illustrators: Gill Bridgewater and Coral Mula
Project design: Alan and Gill Bridgewater
Photography: AG&G Books and Ian Parsons
Editor: Fiona Corbridge
Brickwork: Alan Bridgewater

Reproduction by Pica Digital, Singapore
Printed and bound in Malaysia by Times Offset (M) Sdn. Bhd.

Contents

Part 1: Techniques *8*

Part 2: Projects *32*

Introduction

When we saw our first house – an isolated Victorian farmhouse – we were confronted with numerous red brick outbuildings which were all, to some degree, tumbledown ruins. However, the bricks were crisp and hard-edged, and the lime mortar soft – so much so that we were able to scrape the bricks clean. We decided to salvage bricks from the outbuildings to renovate and extend the main house. We made contact with a retired master bricklayer in the village, who was prepared to give advice.

We spent the next ten years working on our home – Gill scraping the bricks, and our two toddler sons doing their bit. Of course it was hard work, and we made lots of mistakes, but we were spurred on by the excitement of it all. We had the time of our lives building everything from walls and arches through to pillars, posts, raised beds, paths, sheds and even the top half of a well!

The ambition of this book is to share with you all the pleasures of working with brick to create garden features. With each project, we take you through the procedures of considering the design and working out how it might be modified to suit your individual needs. We tell you how to use the tools and materials, and explain the

essential techniques. Illustrations and photographs show how best to achieve the step-by-step procedures; in fact, we take you through all the stages of designing, making, constructing and finishing.

Brickwork doesn't require complex tools or specialized knowledge: it is about working with your hands in the garden, and the pleasure of using your mind and body to create exciting structures.

Best of luck!

HEALTH AND SAFETY

Some of the procedures for making the brickwork projects are hazardous, so before starting work, read the advice below:

• A few projects are physically demanding and if you have doubts about whether you are up to it, get advice from your doctor. When lifting heavy items, minimize back strain by holding the item close to your body, and bend your knees rather than your back.

• Never operate a machine, or attempt a difficult lifting or manoeuvring task, if you are feeling tired.

• Wear gloves and goggles when you are handling and breaking hardcore. Wear gloves, goggles and a dust-mask when mixing cement, using the angle grinder, or cutting bricks with a hammer and chisel.

• Follow manufacturers' instructions when using tools and materials.

• Keep a first-aid kit and telephone nearby, in case of an emergency and, if possible, avoid working alone.

• Do not build a pond if you have young children. Other water features are safer, but even so, never leave children unsupervised.

• Use a safety electricity circuit breaker (between the power socket and the plug) when operating electrical tools and water pumps, to prevent electric shock.

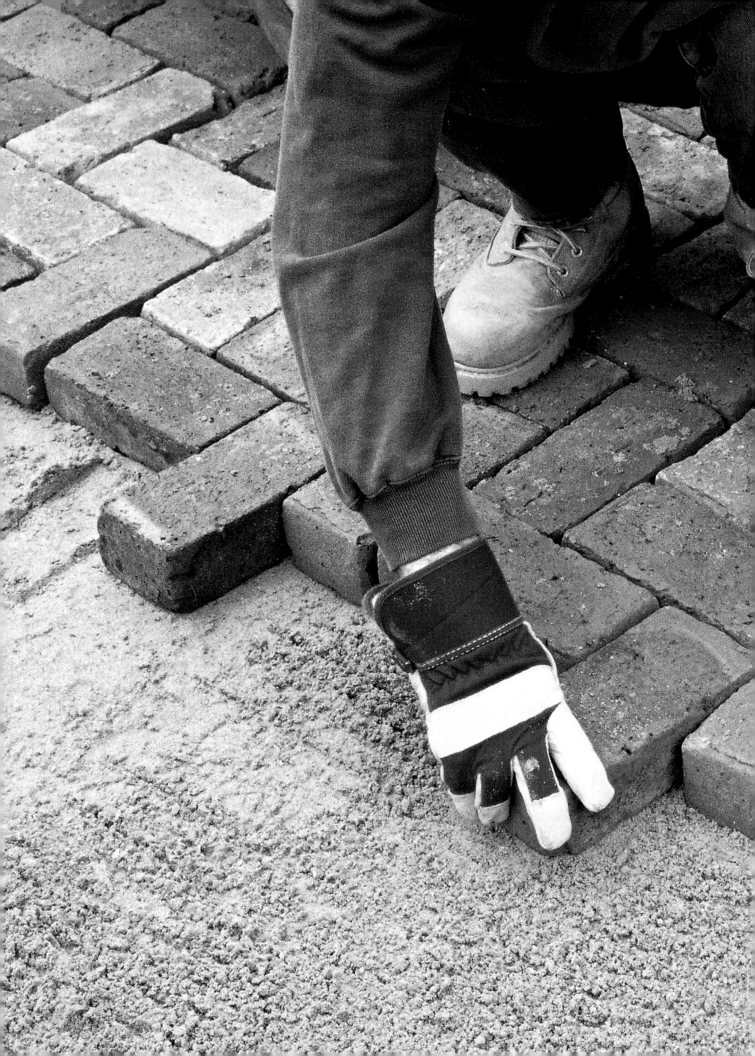

Part 1: Techniques

Design and planning

The art of working with bricks relies on the coordination between mind, hand and eye: the key words are planning, rhythm, repetition and timing. The trick is to fit the components together with the minimum of measuring and as few cuts as possible. If you do have to make a cut, the challenge is to get it right the first time! If you can use the bricks as you find them – new, salvaged, seconds or left over from another job – so much the better.

FIRST CONSIDERATIONS

- What do you want to achieve? Write down the aspects that are important to you, and look at magazines, books and other people's gardens to assess the possibilities. If necessary, change our project designs to suit your needs.
- Bricks are made in many colours and textures. Do some research into what is available, and see what appeals.
- To make a project fit better into your space, you may have to consider changing its size, shape and proportions. Would it, for example, look better as a larger but low, long and thin structure, or as a square rather than round structure? Use the dimensions of a brick to dictate the precise overall project dimensions – working in a number of whole bricks wherever possible. (See pages 24–25 for how to cut bricks.)
- Location and orientation are important. Mark the envisaged position with sticks, plastic sheet or plywood, and look out for possible problems such as the blocking of routes through the garden, unfortunate viewpoints and the casting of shadows.
- If the project is a pond or water feature, does it require a long trench to be dug in the garden to bury a power cable, and is this possible?
- Are there parts of a project's construction that you don't understand? Try working out the problem on paper or mocking up the structure with real materials.
- Calculate the costs and time involved, to make sure that the project is feasible.

Choosing a suitable project

Sometimes it is easy to get carried away and build something massive that dominates the space and quite frankly looks out of place, because the scale is wrong and the style is not suitable. So before you decide what to build, take stock of your garden or courtyard and consider how to improve it. If it is cluttered, you may want to rebuild an existing feature to make it smaller, stronger or more decorative. If the area is a bombsite or a blank canvas, design the whole garden first; when you are ready to build brickwork projects, make sure they fit into the overall scheme.

Garden features are more than basic structures that are constructed out of necessity – they are also decorative. You may need to change the appearance or style of a project to suit your garden. For example, a simple, well-proportioned brick planter

would suit a modern scheme, but for a Victorian garden, it would be more appropriate to incorporate detailing and decoration. From a safety point of view, avoid building ponds and some water features if you have young children.

Planning the project

The first part of a project (and one of the most important) is deciding on its precise size and location. For a patio outside your back door, for example, you need to know its finished height, how it slopes in order to drain rainwater away from the house, and its exact size to the nearest brick and mortar joint.

In the projects in this book, a lot of the planning has been done for you, but do take note of any advice or exceptions that suggest you might need to revise the design, and which refer you to a page within this techniques section. Do a survey of the site and draw simple scaled diagrams on graph paper, showing how the foundation is constructed and how the project is built. Some structures pose more obvious planning problems: steps, for example, have to conform to certain dimensions otherwise you will trip over them; walls that are too high or long can lean or fall down without the benefit of extra support (see pages 29–30).

Every brickwork project requires a foundation: a firm, level (or sometimes slightly sloping, in the case of a patio) base on which to build, otherwise it will collapse. It is very important to use an appropriate foundation, and to plan it in a drawing to show its size and depth. For example, if you want a patio to be level with the surrounding ground, the patio needs to take into account the thickness of the bricks that will be used for paving.

Buying the right tools and materials

Once you have sorted out the project design in detail, you can assess what you need to build it. Sometimes, it is necessary to compromise with both tools and materials in order to make a project affordable. If that is the case, ensure you have enough time to do the work with basic manual tools, and don't resort to inferior materials that will deteriorate quickly.

If you haven't got a wonderful set of tools, consider borrowing or hiring better ones. A cement mixer is worth hiring if you are working on a large project, unless you enjoy body-building exercise! Phone around for quotes for materials, and order in bulk when possible. The choice of bricks available depends on your locality; you can also consider using second-quality bricks (rejects) or reclaimed (second-hand) bricks.

BRICKWORK DESIGNS FOR THE GARDEN

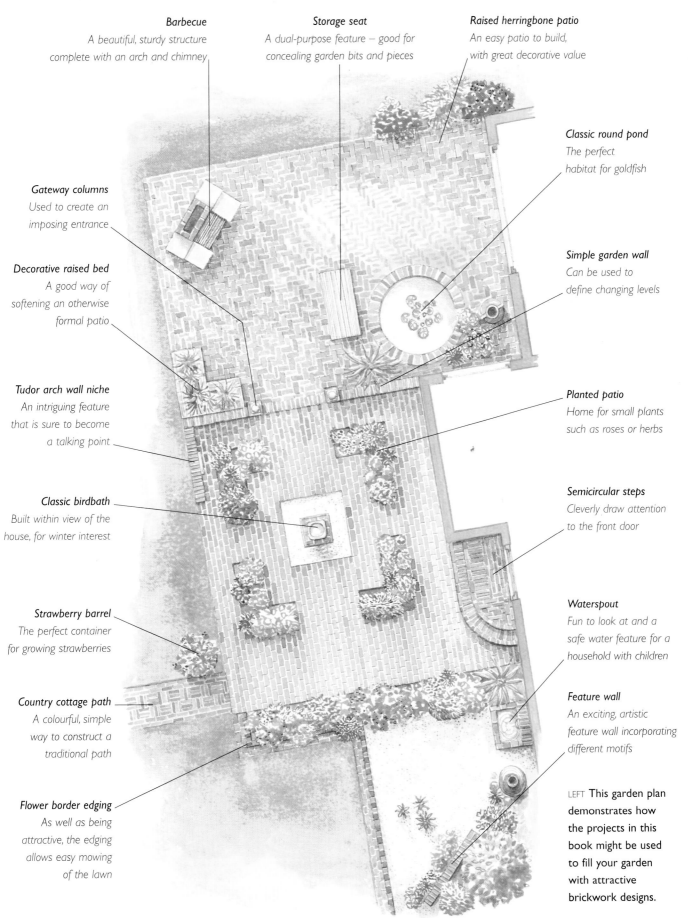

Barbecue
A beautiful, sturdy structure complete with an arch and chimney

Storage seat
A dual-purpose feature – good for concealing garden bits and pieces

Raised herringbone patio
An easy patio to build, with great decorative value

Classic round pond
The perfect habitat for goldfish

Gateway columns
Used to create an imposing entrance

Simple garden wall
Can be used to define changing levels

Decorative raised bed
A good way of softening an otherwise formal patio

Tudor arch wall niche
An intriguing feature that is sure to become a talking point

Planted patio
Home for small plants such as roses or herbs

Classic birdbath
Built within view of the house, for winter interest

Semicircular steps
Cleverly draw attention to the front door

Strawberry barrel
The perfect container for growing strawberries

Waterspout
Fun to look at and a safe water feature for a household with children

Country cottage path
A colourful, simple way to construct a traditional path

Feature wall
An exciting, artistic feature wall incorporating different motifs

Flower border edging
As well as being attractive, the edging allows easy mowing of the lawn

LEFT This garden plan demonstrates how the projects in this book might be used to fill your garden with attractive brickwork designs.

Tools

You don't need many tools for brickwork, but they should be the best tools that you can afford. If you are working to a fixed budget, purchase top-quality trowels (a bricklayer's trowel and a pointing trowel) and a spirit level (a traditional wood-cased one is best), and then save money by buying cheap shovels and suchlike. The following pages describe essential items for the toolbox, and tools you may want to hire to make a job easier.

FOR YOUR OWN PROTECTION

Gloves

Goggles

Dust-mask

Ear defenders

Protecting your hands and feet

Brickwork – digging holes, breaking up hardcore and handling bricks – is tough on your hands, so wear hefty leather gloves whenever possible. You will probably have to take them off for fiddly jobs. When mixing concrete and mortar, wear waterproof, thick rubber gloves, which will protect your skin from contact with corrosive cement powder. Boots made from stout leather, ideally with reinforced metal toecaps, will protect your feet.

More protection

Sometimes it is necessary to wear additional protective gear, especially when you are cutting materials that generate sharp chippings and a lot of dust. Wear goggles when you are smashing hardcore, cutting or breaking bricks, stone and concrete, and a dust-mask when mixing cement powder. When using an angle grinder, wear heavy boots, gloves, goggles, a dust-mask and ear defenders. Wear ear defenders when using any noisy machine.

TOOLS FOR MEASURING AND MARKING

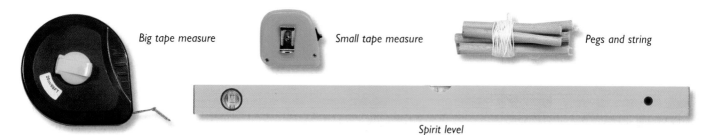

Big tape measure   *Small tape measure*   *Pegs and string*

Spirit level

Measuring and marking out a site

If you are unfamiliar with garden projects and brickwork, it can be difficult to know how to begin. Everything starts from a foundation, so either build on an existing foundation such as a patio (see page 21), or dig out some earth and make a new foundation.

When building a foundation, use a tape measure (available in various lengths) to establish the dimensions, then mark the site with pegs and string (see page 21). If the shape is irregular, use marking chalk or spray paint. Dig out the foundation hole: the sides of the hole contain the foundation. Alternatively, wooden boards (formwork) can be used to construct an accurate frame to retain the foundation. A spirit level is used when digging to a level depth. Spoil should be removed from the site.

Measuring and marking during construction

The exact dimensions of brickwork projects are (or should be) governed by the proportions of a brick (see page 17), so you can either calculate the length and width of the first course, and mark it out on the new or existing foundation using a tape measure, straight-edge and a piece of chalk; or arrange the bricks without mortar, judging the gaps between each brick, then nudge the layout straight and square and mark around it with chalk.

Once you have laid the first course of bricks, use a spirit level to indicate the horizontal and vertical positions, and a straight-edge to check for straightness. A line set (a line stretched between two pegs) is useful for guiding the courses of stone, and estimating course heights, on long lengths of wall (see page 66).

TOOLS FOR MAKING FOUNDATIONS

Sledgehammer

Wheelbarrow

Bucket

Garden rake

Spade   Fork   Shovel

Removing turf and digging earth

Once the area of ground has been marked with string, chalk or paint, start digging and removing earth to create a clean-sided hole of a specific depth. A spade is used to slice through the turf, and a fork is very handy for removing the turf in square chunks. A wheelbarrow is essential for moving earth away from the site, and a bucket is useful for removing small quantities and when working in confined areas. The wheelbarrow and bucket are also employed for moving all other materials. To dig a hole in extremely hard or stony ground, specialist digging tools such as a pickaxe or mattock may be required.

Compacting hardcore

Hardcore (waste brick, stone and concrete) must be compacted in order to form a firm base. A sledgehammer is used to break it up into smaller pieces and to beat these into the ground to make a compact, even layer. This can be notoriously hard work when dealing with large areas (over 2 sq. metres), so either get help or buy broken-brick hardcore, which is easier to break and consolidate. Always wear goggles to protect your eyes from chippings.

Spreading gravel, sand and concrete

Use a shovel for spreading gravel, sand, ballast (a mixture of gravel and sand) and concrete. A rake is useful for spreading dry materials evenly over a large area. A screeding board is brought in to scrape off excess material to make a smooth and level surface to a specific depth, and is used for concrete, sand and ballast. It consists of a length of wood supported at either end by a frame (see page 40). Some patio foundations consist of dry materials, laid down without cement, and it is best to hire a compacting machine called a plate compacter to compress gravel, sand or ballast into a firm base (also for firming patio bricks into position).

TOOLS FOR MIXING CONCRETE AND MORTAR

Mixing by hand

Mixing concrete or mortar by hand is hard work. Find a sheet of exterior plywood for mixing on, about 1.22 m square and 13–25 mm thick, a shovel and a bucket for the water (see pages 22–23). If more than 25 kg of cement or mortar is required, you should seriously consider using a cement mixer.

Using a cement mixer

A cement mixer is used for making concrete and mortar, and is a wonderful timesaver that actually does a better job than you can do by hand. Cement mixers can be bought or hired, and are available in different capacities, powered by an electric or petrol engine. The small, electric versions are most suitable for DIY projects and mix up to approximately twelve shovelfuls of cement, sand or ballast, producing one wheelbarrow load of concrete or mortar. Follow the instructions supplied with the machine. Remember that at the end of a job, an empty cement mixer can only be left for about five minutes before it needs washing out, otherwise the remnants of cement will set solid. Use a hosepipe and a brush to do this.

TOOLS FOR HANDLING MORTAR

Pointing trowel

Bricklayer's trowel

Spreading mortar

The bricklayer's trowel (the larger of the two similarly shaped trowels) is the one used most frequently in bricklaying. It is used to scoop up mortar and spread it smoothly, to an even thickness, over the top and ends of the bricks, and also for slicing off excess mortar that has squeezed out from between the bricks. It can also be employed to knock the bricks level (using the blade or the handle) or to chop bricks roughly in half.

Finishing joints

After the bricks have been laid and before the mortar is dry, the joints between the bricks need to be tidied up with a pointing trowel or by another method (see page 27). The pointing trowel is used to fill any gaps in the joints, and also to repoint (see page 31). Be careful not to smear the excess mortar on the face of the brickwork. The pointing trowel may be used in place of the bricklayer's trowel if you find that too heavy and awkward.

TOOLS FOR CUTTING BRICK, STONE AND CONCRETE

Angle grinder

Bolster chisel

Club hammer   *Mason's hammer*

Cutting bricks

To cut just a few bricks, for the projects in this book, we recommend using hand tools for the sake of simplicity. The most common method is to simply chop the bricks with a bolster chisel and club hammer (see page 24).

Various machines are available for cutting brick and masonry (see page 25). You can use an angle grinder, brick guillotine (good for quick 90° cuts, but the results aren't as good as with a masonry saw), circular saw fitted with an abrasive masonry blade, or a disc cutter fitted with a stone-cutting disc. If your design requires hundreds of bricks to be cut, consider hiring a masonry saw with a diamond blade (which will also cope with angled cuts).

> **CAUTION**
>
> Angle grinders and other hand-held disc cutters are dangerous machines and should only be operated whilst wearing protective gear (see page 25). Follow the manufacturer's advice, and if you have never operated one before, it's advisable to ask an expert or the tool hire shop to show you how to use it safely.

Cutting blocks, slabs, stone and tiles

Concrete block pavers can be cut in the same way as bricks, as described above. Concrete slab pavers, flat pieces of stone and thick concrete or clay tiles can all be cut with a heavyweight disc cutter or masonry saw (depending on size). However, for safety reasons we recommend using a small angle grinder fitted with a stone-cutting disc to score a cut, and then finishing the cut with a bolster chisel and club hammer (see page 24). Most thin tiles can be cut with a basic hand-operated tile-cutting machine.

Wear gloves and goggles when cutting by hand; if using a machine, wear gloves, goggles, a dust-mask, ear defenders and stout boots.

ADDITIONAL TOOLS

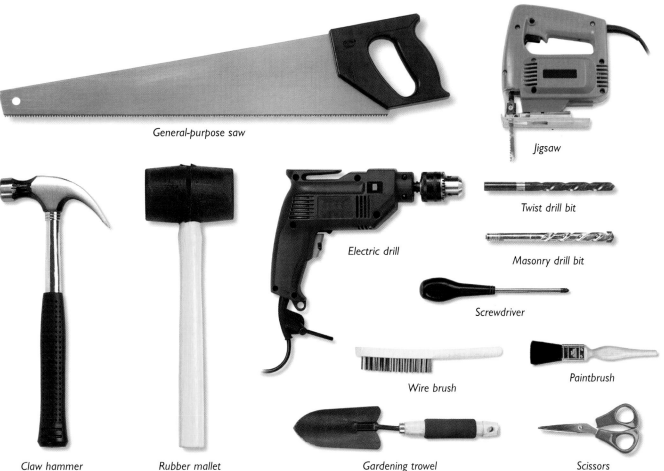

General-purpose saw

Jigsaw

Twist drill bit

Masonry drill bit

Electric drill

Screwdriver

Wire brush

Paintbrush

Claw hammer

Rubber mallet

Gardening trowel

Scissors

Woodwork

Sometimes the projects require you to use formwork (wooden frames) during the casting of foundations. Formwork usually consists of planks of wood laid square and level, held in place by pegs and nails (see page 19). A general-purpose saw (or crosscut saw) and a claw hammer are all that is needed to make it.

Simple brickwork arches are easy to build as long as you use a wooden former to establish the shape of the arch and support the bricks during the building process (see pages 94–99, 108–113, 114–119, 120–125). The former is made from plywood cut with an electric jigsaw, which is a safe and easy-to-use tool. After drawing the curved shape on the plywood (you may use a trammel for this – see page 27), hold down the plywood on the workbench, start up the saw (don't allow the blade to touch the wood until the motor is running) and gently guide the blade around the curve. Wear goggles and follow the manufacturer's instructions.

Drilling holes

A general-purpose electric drill with hammer action is ideal for drilling jobs. For drilling wood, use twist bits for small-diameter holes (under 10 mm in diameter), and flat or spade bits for larger holes. For drilling into brickwork and masonry, use masonry bits and set the drill to hammer mode. Always follow the instructions supplied with the tool.

Finishing

Once you have completed a project (or at the end of each day if you are conscientious), you will need to clear up the site and clean any blobs, splashes and smears of mortar off the brickwork and ground. Use a wire brush to scrub bricks (wear gloves and goggles). If you choose to apply a treatment to the surface of the brickwork in order to clean it (see page 31), use a paintbrush. A paintbrush is also used for any painting tasks such as sealing render with tanking paint, as in the water feature on page 125.

Miscellaneous

A rubber mallet is useful for bedding brickwork or masonry in mortar. It is soft, but heavy, and does the job without damaging the surface of the material. The wooden or plastic-covered handle of a club hammer or mason's hammer will do a similar job. Other useful tools include a screwdriver for driving in screws (if you prefer them to nails) and a gardener's trowel for projects such as the Decorative Raised Bed and the Strawberry Barrel, where planting is required.

When building water features that employ lining materials, such as the Classic Round Pond, use scissors to cut the lining materials; use a hacksaw (a metal saw) to cut the armoured plastic pipe used to protect electric cable and water pipe, in projects such as the Waterspout. Don't buy new tools until the need arises.

Materials

For garden projects, it is best to use well-fired (or high-fired) exterior-grade bricks, or engineering bricks, both of

which are harder than ordinary bricks, with good frost resistance. Your first search, therefore, will be for a supplier

who can provide good-quality bricks at low cost. You can cut costs dramatically by hiring a flat-bed truck and going

to the supplier yourself. If you are lucky, there will be misshapes available at half the normal price – these bruised

and battered bricks are perfect for garden projects. Avoid bricks that show cracks across their width.

BRICKS

Handmade rustic

Handmade facing

Extruded common

Extruded semi-engineering

Header splay

Single bullnose

Angled coping

Half-round coping

"Terracotta" classical panel

Appearance

For most people, the most important aspect of brickwork is its appearance. Generally speaking, bricks are more attractive than other manufactured walling materials such as concrete or reconstituted stone. Use discretion when choosing bricks: some combinations of colour and texture in modern bricks are ugly.

Study examples of finished brickwork to identify the types you like most. Remember the characteristics of a brick are intensified when many bricks are placed together in a wall or patio. Bricks vary from area to area, because they are made from clay dug from the ground, and this varies in colour and properties. They are also manufactured in different ways: machine-made bricks are the most accurately formed and easy to build with; handmade bricks look better but are a bit wobbly and more difficult to lay. The design and availability of special bricks varies according to region.

Properties

Bricks are manufactured for different purposes. "Facing" bricks are sold for their appearance. "Engineering" bricks are intended for situations where high strength and low water absorption are very important, and are not sold for their appearance. This type of brick is the most expensive, and you would probably only choose it for a particular situation, such as when building steps, because its extra strength and hardness guarantee that the edges of the steps will not crumble.

All bricks have a frost-resistance rating, varying from frost resistant, to moderately frost resistant, and not frost resistant (may only be used internally). We have used moderately frost-resistant facing bricks for the projects.

Bricks have six sides: two end or "header" faces, two side or "stretcher" faces, a top or "frog" face, and a bottom face. Most bricks have some kind of cavity to trap mortar – the frog is a rectangular recess in the top for this purpose (some bricks have three holes running right through the brick instead). Bricks with frogs are more versatile, as they have one flat surface that allows them to be used upside down as coping or paving.

Sizes

The dimensions of a brick are significant, and when you start building, you will soon realize why. They are a convenient size to handle, roughly twice as long as they are wide, and their height is roughly one third of their length. This means that they fit together perfectly in many kinds of construction. The precise sizes can vary according to the manufacturer. Imperial and metric bricks may vary, and some bricks are made to match the size of old bricks.

Metric bricks are normally 215 mm long, 102.5 mm wide and 65 mm thick. When calculating the number of bricks required for brickwork, 10 mm mortar joints are allowed for, giving a unit measurement of 225 mm long, 112.5 mm wide and 75 mm thick.

Imperial bricks are normally 9 in long, $4\frac{3}{8}$ in wide and $2\frac{15}{16}$ in thick. Allowing for $\frac{1}{4}$ in mortar joints, this gives a unit measurement of $9\frac{1}{4}$ in long, $4\frac{5}{8}$ in wide and $3\frac{3}{16}$ in thick.

All the projects can be built using metric or imperial bricks, although if imperial bricks are used, the overall finished dimensions will be different to those specified.

Other kinds of brick

If you want to use old bricks from a salvage yard, because you like their antique appearance, or want to match existing brickwork, be prepared to pay more than for new bricks. Avoid bricks with mortar still stuck to them, because it is tough work to chisel off.

"Seconds" (second quality) are bricks that are less than perfect – usually chipped, warped, cracked or damaged by under- or over-firing. Avoid cracked or under-fired bricks.

Many special brick shapes are available for specific and decorative purposes – see what's on offer and consider incorporating these into your projects to give added interest.

BUYING TIPS

- Never buy bricks without inspecting the product.
- When buying seconds, ideally it is best to select each brick individually.
- If you are hiring a truck to collect the bricks yourself, it is much better to make several journeys with small loads, rather than a single journey with an overloaded vehicle.
- If you are having bricks delivered, plan in advance where they are to be unloaded, and make sure that they are not going to pose a hazard or obstruction.

FOUNDATION MATERIALS, MORTAR AND RENDER

Ballast   *Gravel*   *Sharp sand*   *Soft sand*   *Cement*

Concrete, aggregates and ballast

Most foundations begin with hardcore – waste brick, stone and concrete, which is broken into pieces and compacted to provide a firm, interlocked base that allows water drainage. Normally, the foundation is completed with a layer of concrete.

Concrete consists of Portland cement powder, fine aggregate (sand), coarse aggregate (gravel or crushed stone), and water. The shape and size of the particles of sand and stone in the aggregate decide the character of the concrete – its strength, hardness, durability and porosity. Ready-mixed aggregate can be bought in most builders' merchants. This mix of aggregates (sharp sand and small stones or gravel) is often called ballast. For the projects, pick an average mix made up from small-sized gravel and sand.

Some foundations for patios and paths omit the concrete – alternative foundations are: hardcore, gravel and sand; hardcore and ballast; or hardcore, ballast and sand. In each case, the hardcore, ballast and sand are compacted.

Sand

Sand is available in various types. Sharp sand is coarse and is often used for making concrete, laying under paving, or is mixed with cement to make mortar for rendering (see below). Soft sand (also known as builder's sand) is a medium sand used for making mortar. It can also be used for concrete and foundations (it is not as effective as sharp sand, but you may want to order one type of sand in bulk to do the whole job). Fine sand (also known as silver sand or kiln-dried sand) is ideal for filling the joints in brick and block paving (but use ordinary sand for large gaps).

Mortar

Mortar is a mixture of soft sand, cement powder and water, and is used to stick bricks together. The ratio of ingredients is important and mixing takes practice (see pages 22–23). A mortar made with sharp sand produces a coarser mortar suitable for rendering. Render is a thin coating of mortar stuck to the surface of bricks.

TILES, STONE AND PAVERS

Roof tile

Floor tile

Decorative glazed tile

Clay block paver

Concrete paving slab

Reconstituted stone paving slab

Millstone

Real stone slab

York stone

Roof stone

Real stone block

Cobbles

Boulder

Pebbles

Tiles

A huge range of tiles is available. Clay roof tiles are traditionally used as a coping to finish the top of brickwork structures and help deflect rainwater away from the structure. Decorative clay tiles, designed specifically for brickwork, can be obtained from specialist suppliers. (Those that display a floral decoration are sometimes known as rose blocks.) Some concrete tiles are described as reconstituted stone, because they are made to look like real clay or stone. Terracotta floor tiles, quarry tiles, brightly coloured tiles or patterned glazed tiles can all be incorporated into brickwork to make a decorative design.

Stone

Stone is traditionally combined with brick for decorative effect. Many kinds of real stone are available, but it is often best to choose a type that is quarried in your area, because it will harmonize with the colour of local bricks. See what your supplier has in stock and look at local examples of building to help you choose. Avoid stone that looks crumbly or cracked. Try to select pieces that can be used as they stand, in order to avoid having to cut them. (If cutting is necessary, see pages 24–25.)

Cobbles and pebbles may be bedded in mortar to create a patterned surface that complements brickwork or paving.

Paving slabs

Straightforward concrete paving slabs may be too plain for garden projects, but there are many attractive alternatives. Textured and coloured slabs, or reconstituted stone slabs (a mixture of crushed stone and concrete) can look as good as real stone. Real stone paving slabs are wonderful, but extremely expensive, so your budget may not be able to accommodate them.

Pavers

You can use ordinary bricks for paving (to match nearby brickwork), but the cavities (frogs or holes) will need filling with sand and the bricks cannot be laid with equal gaps between them, because their proportions are designed to incorporate mortar joints – however, this sometimes adds to their charm.

Pavers (or paviors) are extremely hard, thin clay or concrete bricks designed specifically for paths, patios and drives. They come in many shapes, sizes and finishes. Perhaps the most attractive and durable option is the kiln-fired, brick-sized clay paver, in subtle colours that never fade. (Concrete pavers fade in colour after five to ten years.) Pavers are exactly twice as long as they are wide, and are usually thinner than a brick, which makes them easier to lay in patterns. The recess required to lay them is shallower than that needed for bricks. Concrete pavers include imitation stone setts (small rectangular paving blocks), and mock bricks.

WOOD AND PLYWOOD

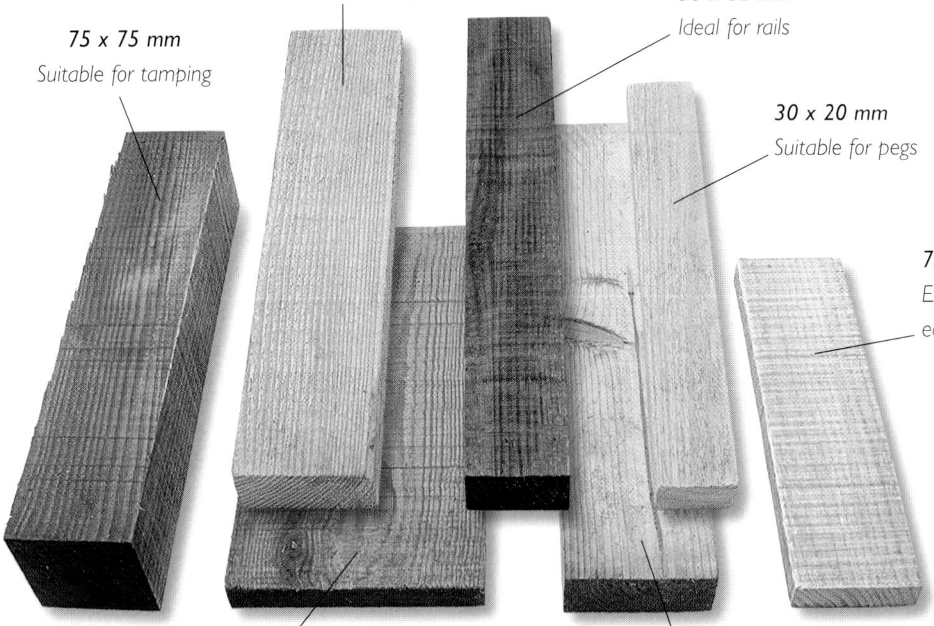

75 x 75 mm
Suitable for tamping

70 x 30 mm
Good for framing

50 x 32 mm
Ideal for rails

30 x 20 mm
Suitable for pegs

75 x 20 mm
Excellent for edging paths

Plywood

150 x 20 mm
Suitable for formwork

Useful timber sections

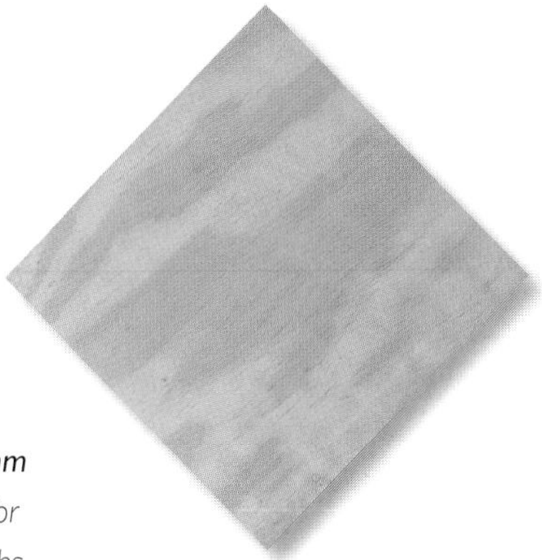

90 x 40 mm
Good for edging small slabs

Sleeper

Formwork

Formwork is the wooden framing used to make a foundation. Use cheap, ready-sawn or reclaimed wood, as it will be ruined by the cement and usually serves no purpose after the foundation is complete. Plywood consists of thin layers of wood stuck together, and is ideal for making formers, which are the arched frames used to support brickwork arches during construction. It comes in standard-size sheets of 2.44 x 1.22 m, or smaller pieces cut from it.

Other uses

Wood goes well with brick – the warm colours look good together. Treated pine, oak or railway sleepers can be incorporated into your garden projects.

During the construction process, cheap exterior-grade plywood (often called "shuttering" plywood) can be used to protect the area surrounding a project, guarding lawns and drives against general mess and damage.

MISCELLANEOUS

Some projects in this book, especially the Classic Round Pond and the Waterspout, use a wider range of materials than shown here. Specialist materials such as geo-textile and butyl will probably not be available at your DIY superstore. Look up suppliers in a directory of businesses in your area (geo-textile and butyl are sold by suppliers of pond-building materials and water features).

Foundations

When it comes to building foundations, you can't cut costs. Most projects need a solid, no-nonsense concrete foundation. If you suspect that the conditions in your garden mean that a stronger than average foundation is required, adjustments to the basic foundation can be made. For example, if the ground is soft, simply make the foundation wider and deeper, or if the ground is very wet, lay extra hardcore to increase drainage.

ABOUT FOUNDATIONS

Every brickwork project requires a foundation of some kind. A foundation is a strong, stable, level base on which to build. It would be no good laying bricks directly on the ground, because their weight, together with rainwater, would compress and erode the soil causing the brick structure to sink, crack, lean over and fall apart. So whether you are constructing a wall, a birdbath or a patio, start by building a good foundation. Foundations are usually made from hardcore topped by concrete. Foundations for patios and paths often omit the concrete and substitute other materials. Sometimes it is possible to use an existing foundation (see box).

TYPES OF FOUNDATION

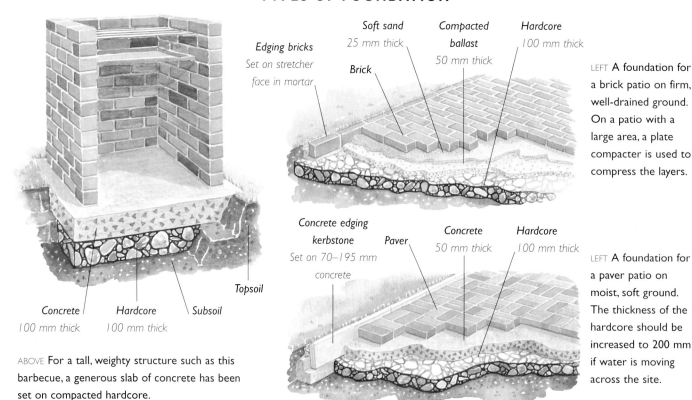

Edging bricks
Set on stretcher face in mortar

Soft sand
25 mm thick

Brick

Compacted ballast
50 mm thick

Hardcore
100 mm thick

LEFT **A foundation for a brick patio on firm, well-drained ground. On a patio with a large area, a plate compacter is used to compress the layers.**

Concrete edging kerbstone
Set on 70–195 mm concrete

Paver

Concrete
50 mm thick

Hardcore
100 mm thick

LEFT **A foundation for a paver patio on moist, soft ground. The thickness of the hardcore should be increased to 200 mm if water is moving across the site.**

Topsoil

Concrete
100 mm thick

Hardcore
100 mm thick

Subsoil

ABOVE **For a tall, weighty structure such as this barbecue, a generous slab of concrete has been set on compacted hardcore.**

Most brickwork walls, and upright structures such as barbecues and planters, need a strong hardcore and concrete foundation as illustrated above left.

For paving projects – patios and paths – the foundation can consist of hardcore and a dryish mix of concrete or, alternatively, hardcore and compacted layers of other materials (although not as solid as concrete, this foundation is adequate for domestic patios and paths, and less work to make). This alternative foundation can be made of hardcore, gravel and sand; hardcore and ballast; or hardcore, ballast and sand. In each case, the hardcore, ballast and sand are compacted. However, if the ground is soft, sandy or boggy, it is better to include concrete in the foundation. Also, if the design of the project means that it will be awkward to use the plate compacter required for compacting the materials, opt for a concrete foundation. Edging bricks or blocks need to be stuck down with mortar or contained by a kerb.

MEASURING, MARKING AND DIGGING

Pegs
Arrange the pegs as shown so that the string crosses at the corners

Square
A square ensures 90° corners

Central peg

String
Use the string to mark out the foundation

Dimensions
Check the dimensions with a tape measure

Taut string
Radius of circle

Scribbling peg

Resultant circle
Marked with chalk

ABOVE Pegs, string and a tape measure (a square may also be useful) are used to mark out a rectangular area of the correct size.

ABOVE The method for marking out a circular foundation, using two pegs and a length of string, plus some chalk.

Work out the exact size of the foundation (for example, although a patio foundation is the same size as the finished patio, a wall foundation needs to be wider than a wall) and its precise depth. To establish the depth, survey the site (if the ground slopes, knock a peg in the ground to indicate the chosen finished level of the foundation) and draw a cross-section of the construction (visualize the project sliced across the middle with a knife) to help calculate the depth of soil that should be removed.

Mark out rectangular areas using pegs, string and a tape measure. If the foundation is an L-shape or other complex shape, divide it into a series of rectangles. To check the accuracy of a rectangle, make sure the opposite sides are of equal length, then measure the diagonals, add them together and divide by two. This tells you how long a diagonal should be in a shape with 90° corners. To make the diagonals equal, adjust the pegs' positions.

For circular foundations, bang a peg into the ground at the centre. Make a length of string with a loop at each end (the length from loop to loop should be the same as the radius of the circle). Slip one loop over the central peg, insert another peg into the other end and use it to scribe out a circle. Mark the circle using spray paint, chalk powder or chalk. Dig out the foundation as described on page 13.

LAYING FOUNDATIONS

The initial layer of most foundations consists of hardcore, which is broken and compacted with a sledgehammer to make a firm base. The second layer of a foundation for upright structures, such as a wall or barbecue, is usually concrete. Wooden formwork is normally laid to contain it. Pegs are nailed to the outer side of boards and knocked through the hardcore into the ground, so that they are level with each other. The boards indicate where the top of the concrete should be. When the concrete is laid, a length of wood is used to scrape away excess concrete and tamp it level. For many paving projects, the second layer might consist of gravel, followed by a layer of sand compacted to just below the finished level of the foundation. This is topped with loose sand. (For foundations larger then 3 m in either direction, divide up the area with extra boards set to the finished height of the foundation.)

Concrete
The concrete is cast to the level of the boards

Formwork
Wooden boards are used to set the level of the concrete

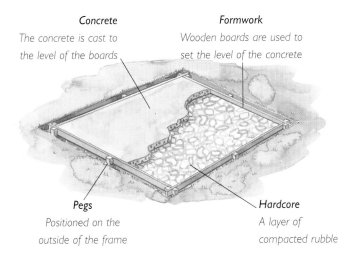

Pegs
Positioned on the outside of the frame

Hardcore
A layer of compacted rubble

ABOVE This foundation is designed to be set flush with the ground. A formwork frame is used to contain the concrete.

USING EXISTING FOUNDATIONS

If a brickwork feature is small, it is sometimes possible to build it on an existing area of paving. Before you do that, if possible check what is underneath the paving by lifting a few bricks, blocks or slabs. If the foundation looks poor, lift the paving in the area you need to build on, dig out extra earth and make a proper foundation, replacing the original paving afterwards. Once you are satisfied that the area is solid, check that it is level. Small discrepancies can be compensated for by adding extra mortar under the first course of bricks. If the slope is too great (more than 10 mm across the length of the brickwork), cast a level concrete slab on top, no less than 40 mm thick, on which to build.

Concrete and mortar

Concrete and mortar are two very important components in brickwork construction. Concrete is used in foundations and mortar is used to stick bricks together, and for rendering. They are both made from mixing dry ingredients, including cement powder, with water. For successful mixtures, it is important to get the right ratio of ingredients and correct amount of water. For the most part, you can use a shovel to measure out dry ingredients.

ABOUT CONCRETE AND MORTAR

At first, you may look at a concrete or mortar mix and wonder how it is going to work, but it will set solid overnight and gain strength slowly over a few days. Mortar needs to be soft and buttery, so that it slices and cuts, and stays where it has been put without oozing or dribbling. However, the exact consistency required will depend on the absorbency of the bricks, and the humidity of the weather on the day. As with cooking the perfect loaf, follow the recipe to the letter, but be ready to make adjustments to suit changing needs. If the weather is dry, spray the bricks and mortar with a fine mist of water as you work.

MIXING METHODS FOR CONCRETE AND MORTAR

> **CAUTION**
>
> Cement and lime are corrosive and can seriously burn the skin. Always wear goggles and gloves, and wash your hands and face after working with them.

For quantities that require in excess of 25 kg of cement powder, we recommend that you hire a cement mixer.

Mixing in a wheelbarrow

1 Use a shovel to measure out the dry ingredients into the wheelbarrow – first the sand or ballast, and then the cement. Continue until you have enough or the barrow is half-full. Turn the ingredients over several times until they are thoroughly mixed.
2 Pour about one-third of a bucket of water into one end of the wheelbarrow, then drag small amounts of the dry ingredients into the water. Repeat the process until all the water has been soaked up by the dry ingredients.
3 Turn over the whole heap several times, all the while adding small amounts of water, until you can chop it into clean, wet slices.

Mixing on a board

1 Measure the dry ingredients on to a board with a shovel – first the sand or ballast, then the cement. Mix until it is an even colour.
2 Dig a hole in the centre and pour in about half a bucket of water. Work round the heap, dragging small amounts of the dry materials into the water. If the water threatens to break over the rim, swiftly pull in more of the dry materials to stem the flow.
3 When the water has been soaked up, add more until the concrete or mortar is the correct consistency. The finished mixture should form crisp, firm slices that stand up under their own weight without crumbling.

Mixing
Drag the dry materials into the water

ABOVE It is often convenient to use a wheelbarrow for mixing mortar; remember to give it a good clean afterwards.

Mixing
Make a hole in the heap and add a small amount of water

ABOVE When mixing on a board, drag the dry materials into the water in the centre of the heap. Try not to let the water escape.

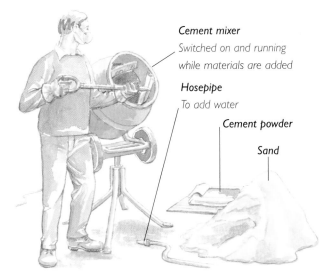

ABOVE Use a shovel to measure quantities, for example one shovelful (1 part) of cement powder to four shovelfuls (4 parts) of sand.

Mixing using a cement mixer

Follow the instructions supplied with the machine and use an electricity circuit breaker safety device between the plug and socket. Measure out the sand or ballast using a shovel, switch on the mixer and put it straight into the machine. Don't overfill: a small machine can take about 10–12 shovelfuls (including cement powder). Add the cement. After a few minutes, when the ingredients are evenly mixed, start adding water a little at a time, until the correct consistency is achieved. (See box on recipes.)

GENERAL HANDLING OF CONCRETE AND MORTAR

It is best to use buckets to move a small quantity of concrete or mortar, and a wheelbarrow for large amounts. Make sure that the load is balanced. Two half-buckets are easier to move than one bucket that is full to overflowing. The same goes for a wheelbarrow: it's easier to move two small loads than it is to move a barrow that is so full that it slops and spills when you jolt over a bump. In most instances, a shovel is the best tool for unloading your cargo, although a small spade is good for filling up buckets.

WEATHER CONDITIONS

Concrete and mortar like to cure slowly – the longer the better. If the weather is anything other than cool and damp, then to a lesser or greater extent you need to protect both concrete and mortar. If you have just built a wall and it's so hot that you can see the mortar drying out, cover it with damp newspaper. If the sun is blazing down on newly-laid concrete, cover it with wet sacking and spray it at regular intervals over the next day or so. If you are expecting a night frost, cover both concrete and mortar with dry sacking, layers of newspaper or sheets of plastic. If it starts to rain heavily, cover everything with sheets of plastic.

CONCRETE AND MORTAR RECIPES

Ingredients are measured by volume (in the projects, weights are given only as a guide to ordering materials, since volumes of different materials vary in weight, and sand and ballast are heavier when wet). "Parts" signify the ratios of ingredients (by volume) to each other, measured in the same manner (such as by the shovelful). So a recipe listing 1 part cement and 4 parts sand, means 1 shovelful of cement and 4 shovelfuls of sand, or 2 shovelfuls of cement and 8 shovelfuls of sand, depending on the quantity you are mixing. Recipes do vary, but we recommend that you use the following proportions.

Concrete for foundations

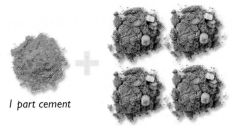

1 part cement

4 parts ballast

Mix 1 part cement with 4 parts ballast. Add water and mix to the consistency of stiff mashed potatoes. You can substitute 2 parts sharp sand and 3 parts aggregate for the 4 parts ballast. (You may wish to do this if you have bought these materials in bulk and want to use them instead of ordering ballast.)

Dryish mix of concrete for paving foundations

As above, except that a lot less water is added – just enough to damp down the dry ingredients. The mixture will absorb moisture from the air and set after a few days.

Mortar for bricklaying and pointing

1 part cement

4 parts soft sand

Mix 1 part cement with 4 parts soft sand. Add water and mix to the consistency of mashed potatoes. For exposed sites where strong winds and heavy rain may erode the mortar, 1 part cement and 3 parts sand is commonly used.

Dryish mix of mortar for paving joints

As above, except a lot less water is added (add water as described for dryish mix of concrete).

Cutting brick, stone and concrete

In many ways, the sign of a good brickworker is the ability to place bricks for best fit without having to cut many of them. When you do need to make a cut, it must be accurate. For the most part, you will be using a club hammer and bolster chisel to cut bricks into halves and quarters. To cut concrete slabs and tiles, it might be necessary to use an electric angle grinder. Clay tiles can be cut with a heavy-duty ceramic tile cutter.

CUTTING BRICKS

HOW TO AVOID TOO MUCH CUTTING

- Plan the length and width of the structure – path or wall – so that it is made up from a number of whole bricks.
- If you are using a mixture of materials – such as bricks and tiles, or bricks and concrete slabs – make sure that the module sizes of each are compatible.
- Avoid using a mixture of imperial and metric bricks, unless there is a good reason to do so.
- Choose a bond that works without the need to cut bricks.
- Go for structures that are rectilinear in plan view, rather than triangular or hexagonal, for example.
- If you want to use a bond that requires bricks to be cut, at least choose one that only requires you to cut bricks in half.

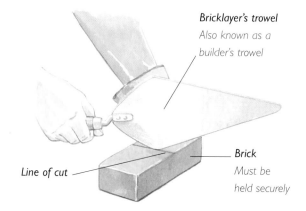

Bricklayer's trowel
Also known as a builder's trowel

Brick
Must be held securely

Line of cut

ABOVE Give the brick a firm, well-placed blow with the edge of the bricklayer's trowel and it should fall in two.

Cutting bricks with a bricklayer's trowel or mason's hammer

The most basic way of cutting a brick is with a bricklayer's trowel: hold the brick in one hand and strike it firmly with the edge of the trowel. If you are lucky, the brick will fall in half. If it doesn't, repeat the procedure on the other face.

To use a mason's hammer, simply hold the brick in one hand – so that the waste end is pointing away from your body – and then use the chisel end of the mason's hammer to clip away at the waste until you have cut back to the mark. Work little by little, backing up to the line of cut.

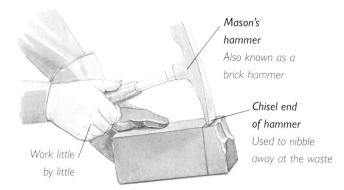

Mason's hammer
Also known as a brick hammer

Chisel end of hammer
Used to nibble away at the waste

Work little by little

ABOVE Work with a pecking action, gradually nibbling back the brick to the marked line of cut.

Cutting bricks with a bolster chisel

A more accurate way of cutting bricks is by using a club hammer and bolster chisel. This is the method used most frequently in small brickwork projects. Position the brick on something soft, such as a pad of old carpet, or on the lawn, to help absorb the shock of the blow. Wear goggles and strong leather gloves. Take the bolster chisel in one hand and the club hammer in the other, and set the edge of the chisel firmly on the line of cut, so that it is upright and square with the brick. Finally, give the chisel a single, well-placed blow with the hammer and the brick should fall in half. It may be wise to practise on some old bricks first.

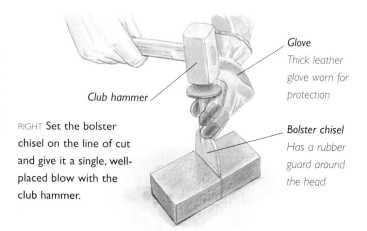

Glove
Thick leather glove worn for protection

Club hammer

Bolster chisel
Has a rubber guard around the head

RIGHT Set the bolster chisel on the line of cut and give it a single, well-placed blow with the club hammer.

Cutting bricks with a machine

There are various machines you can use to cut bricks:

• Angle grinder fitted with a stone-cutting disc (see page 14).

• Brick guillotine. To use a guillotine cutter, mark the brick where you want to cut it and place it on the platform below the chisel-like blade. Pull down on the lever.

• Circular saw fitted with a masonry blade (hand-held power tool). Use in the same way as an angle grinder.

• Disc cutter fitted with a stone-cutting disc (a disc cutter normally describes a large angle grinder). To use, follow the instructions for an angle grinder (see below).

• Masonry saw. To use a masonry saw, place the machine on a level surface, set the brick on the platform, so that the line of cut is aligned with the marking guide, and then pull down on the lever so that the disc makes the cut.

• Machines are potentially dangerous – follow the manufacturer's instructions carefully and always wear goggles, a dust-mask and gloves. Ear defenders and stout boots are also recommended.

CUTTING TILES, STONE AND CONCRETE

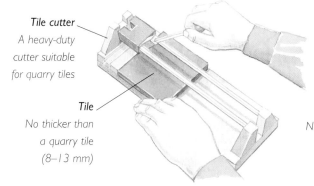

Tile cutter
A heavy-duty cutter suitable for quarry tiles

Tile
No thicker than a quarry tile (8–13 mm)

ABOVE Having scored the line of cut, draw the handle back so that the anvil is centred on the tile, and press down on the lever.

Tiles

Clay tiles – roof tiles and quarry tiles – are best cut with a good-quality, heavy-duty ceramic tile cutter. All you do is butt the tile hard up against the stop, so that the line of cut is aligned with the handle, and then push the lever forward so that the little wheel scores the surface of the tile. Then you pull the lever back so that the anvil is bridged over the tile, and push down hard so that the tile snaps in half. Clear the debris after every cut.

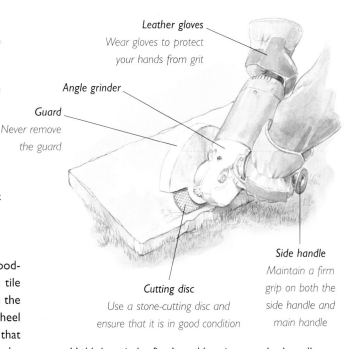

Leather gloves
Wear gloves to protect your hands from grit

Angle grinder

Guard
Never remove the guard

Side handle
Maintain a firm grip on both the side handle and main handle

Cutting disc
Use a stone-cutting disc and ensure that it is in good condition

ABOVE Hold the grinder firmly, and keeping your body well away from the line of cut, make repeated light passes to cut a groove.

> **CAUTION**
>
> Angle grinders always produce a hail of splinters and dust. Goggles and a dust-mask must be worn at all times. Ear defenders, strong gloves and sturdy boots are also recommended.

Cutting stone and concrete with an angle grinder

Set the slab flat on the lawn and use a tape measure and chalk to draw out the line of cut. Put on goggles, a dust-mask, ear defenders and gloves. Hold the grinder so that the wheel is at right angles to the slab. Brace yourself, switch on the power and gently run the spinning disc forward, to lightly score along the marked cut. Make several runs to deepen the line of cut, then switch off the power and flip the slab over. Switch the power back on and re-run the whole procedure on the other side. Continue repeating the process until the slab of stone or concrete falls in two. During the whole cutting operation, always make sure that both you and the power cable remain well clear of the cutting disc. Always use a circuit breaker.

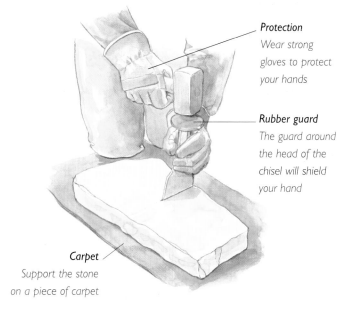

Protection
Wear strong gloves to protect your hands

Rubber guard
The guard around the head of the chisel will shield your hand

Carpet
Support the stone on a piece of carpet

ABOVE Cutting stone using a bolster chisel and club hammer. Hold the chisel firmly on the mark and deliver a well-aimed blow.

Bricklaying

There can be something truly calming and therapeutic about bricklaying. The trick is to make sure that everything is well prepared, with the piles of bricks comfortably to hand, and the mortar at the ready, so that your rhythm of work is not broken. It is perfectly possible to cope with the work on your own, but if you can find a willing helper to pile up the bricks and mix the mortar, so much the better.

PLANNING THE COURSES

Walls and box structures

To build a wall, allow 10 mm between each brick for mortar, and lay out a line of bricks to fit your chosen measurement in the best way. (If you are building a box structure, measure out the next side and repeat the procedure already described.) Lay the second course on the first so that the vertical joints are staggered. Working in this way, you will be able to plan out the structure without the need to cut bricks.

Circles, curves and arches

Let's say that you want to build a circle or curve of bricks with a 1 m radius. Take two

ABOVE Plan out the initial two courses of a box structure first.

ABOVE Half-bricks with tiles (left) and bricks set on edge (right).

wooden pegs and link them with string, so that they are 1 m apart. Bang one peg in the ground, and use the other peg to indicate the circle. Lay the bricks (dry) around the circumference of the circle. When you come to the last brick, make adjustments to the gaps between each brick in the whole circle, to achieve a good fit. (The fit of the bricks can be planned on a scaled drawing, if you wish.) You may like to consider using half-bricks, or bricks laid on their stretcher (side) face, to create curved structures. If you are building an arch, plan it out on the ground before you start work, in order to avoid mistakes.

BASIC PROCEDURES

Setting out the line

Determine the line of the wall by banging in a peg at each end of the concrete foundation. Take a length of string and run it over a piece of chalk, or through a container of chalk powder. Stretch the line between the pegs, a few millimetres above the ground, tying it so that it is taut and flush with the ground. When you are happy that the line is marking the course of the wall, lift it between finger and thumb and let it go with a snap, so that it slaps down a line of chalk on the concrete. (Alternatively, use a simple device called a chalk line, containing replaceable chalk, which deposits chalk on a string as you pull it out of the container.)

Applying mortar

Spread a line of mortar about 12 mm thick and 300 mm long, and draw the point of the trowel through it to make a valley. Set the first brick in place and tap it with the handle of the trowel so that the excess squeezes out, and the mortar joint is about 10 mm thick. Use the point of the trowel to push the excess mortar up on to the end of the brick to form the vertical joint, and then lay the second brick. Continue in this way until the end of the row. Check each course for height, and use the spirit level vertically, horizontally and diagonally to check that all the bricks are in line.

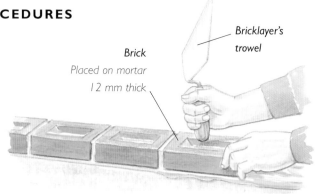

Brick
Placed on mortar 12 mm thick

Bricklayer's trowel

ABOVE Set the brick carefully in place on the mortar and tap it level with the handle of the bricklayer's trowel.

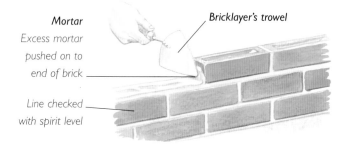

Mortar
Excess mortar pushed on to end of brick

Bricklayer's trowel

Line checked with spirit level

ABOVE There are several ways to apply mortar – this is just one of them. It is a good method for beginners.

THINGS TO AVOID

- On a hot day, don't use bricks dry: always dampen them so that they feel slightly less absorbent to the touch.
- Don't immediately scrape off excess mortar as it oozes out from between the bricks, because you will mark the bricks. It is much better to leave it until the bricks have absorbed the water from the mortar, and then scrape it off with the trowel.
- Don't use sharp sand, dirty sand or stale cement to make mortar; use soft sand and fresh cement.
- Don't let the mortar on the trowels and spirit level dry out – wash them every half hour or so.

ADDITIONAL TECHNIQUES

If you are finding it difficult to keep a uniform thickness of mortar between the joints when building a wall, a gauge rod will help. In effect, this is a batten marked off along its length with alternate thicknesses for bricks and joints – 65 mm for the height or thickness of the brick, 10 mm for the thickness of the mortar, then 65 mm, 10 mm, 65 mm and so on along the batten. Simply stand this against the wall being built and use it to assess your progress, then make necessary adjustments by knocking the bricks harder or by adding more mortar.

Never assume that you can make mistakes here and there and make good at the end – you can't. It is important to be consistent and make sure that every brick is placed well.

USING A TRAMMEL

A trammel is used when building circles or circle-based curves. It usually consists of a length of wood (trammel arm) drilled at one end, a block of wood the thickness of a brick (trammel support block), and a sheet of plywood (base). The support block is positioned on the base, surrounded by bricks to keep it in place. The trammel arm pivots on a

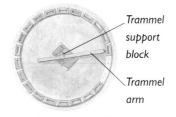

Trammel support block

Trammel arm

ABOVE If desired, a nail can be fixed to the arm as a pointer.

nail hammered into the trammel support block. Each brick is placed so that it is aligned with the centre of the circle, and so that it just touches the end of the arm. A u-shaped piece may be fixed to the arm to indicate the position of the edge bricks, which are laid to meet the end of the trammel at 90°. There are also slightly different versions of the trammel.

POINTING

ABOVE The joints between bricks need to be filled neatly with mortar. Use the edge of the trowel to wipe the mortar into the joint. Approach from both sides in order to create a peaked effect (mason's joint).

"Pointing" describes the finishing of the mortar joint between the bricks. There are four common finishes: raked or keyed, mason's, flat or flush, and weathered or struck. Pointing is done as the bricks are laid (avoid if the mortar is wet and sloppy), or when the wall is complete.

Raked joints are created by using a round bar, trowel handle or another tool to run along the joint in order to hollow it. When using old bricks to build walls in the garden, the best finish is a raked joint: wait until the end of the day, and then use the point of the pointing trowel to swiftly rake the joint clear of excess mortar. This finish is perfect for a rustic cottage garden wall.

A mason's joint is formed by wiping the mortar into a peak. Flush joints are made by using the edge of the trowel to scrape the mortar off flush with the bricks. In a weathered joint, the mortar is scraped out at an angle.

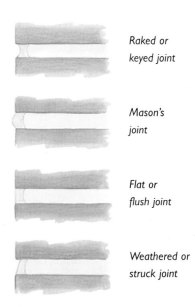

Raked or keyed joint

Mason's joint

Flat or flush joint

Weathered or struck joint

INCORPORATING OTHER MATERIALS

In times past, bricks walls were traditionally less uniform affairs, with bricks of varying thickness and much thicker joints. In some areas, it was common to stud wide joints with little pieces of stone or broken tiles. Rather than going to the trouble of cutting or rubbing bricks to create shaped bricks for arches, it was quite usual to use a stack of roof tiles or old quarry tiles to fill the space. In some coastal areas, it was common to stud joints with shells. Some builders incorporated specially shaped bricks.

Brick bonds and patterns

The pattern created by placing bricks to form a continuous wall, or laying them to form a patio surface, is known as the bond. The secret of creating a sound brick wall lies in the vertical joints of neighbouring courses – these must be staggered. If vertical joints are not staggered, the structural integrity of the brickwork is at risk. There are various traditional bonds that achieve this. Look around your area for examples of brick patterns.

BASIC BONDS FOR WALLS AND STRUCTURES

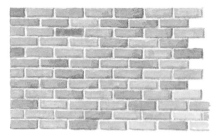

Stretcher bond

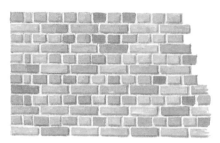

English bond

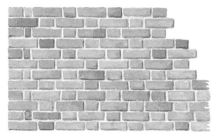

Flemish bond

The three primary bonds are stretcher bond, English bond and Flemish bond. In a stretcher bond, each course is formed entirely of stretchers (side face of the brick), and it is only suitable for walls 102.5 mm (half a brick) thick. Each brick half-laps half its length on the bricks in the course below. A stretcher bond is great when you only want to build a low structure or a cavity wall.

In an English bond, alternate courses show headers (end face of the brick) and stretchers. The end or head of the brick is centred on the middle of the stretcher in the course below.

Flemish bond consists of alternate headers and stretchers in each course, with headers always being placed over the centre of the stretcher below. Less common bonds are shown on the right.

SPECIAL BONDS

English garden wall bond

Heading bond

Flemish garden wall bond

Honeycomb bond

PATTERNS

Patterns on walls

Different coloured bricks can be used to create a pattern, as in the English diaper tradition (an all-over surface decoration of a small repeated pattern such as diamonds or squares, using coloured, projecting or recessed bricks). The way bricks are arranged can also create a pattern – either a self-pattern, as with a herringbone panel, or together with tiles.

Diaper pattern (darker colour)

Diaper pattern (lighter colour)

Patterns on patios and paths

Patterns for patios and paths are created in much the same way as for walls, by brick colour or arrangement. Because there are not the same concerns about structural integrity as for a wall, you can introduce additional elements, such as stones and shells, to create pattern, or use different thicknesses of brick.

Herringbone band course

Raking tile courses

Walls and other structures

Brick walls are all around us – but next time you are out walking, notice how arches, columns, piers and pillars can be used to lift a structure out of the ordinary, with a unique coming together of beauty and function. At its most basic, a brick wall can be one brick thick, just two or three courses high, and built on an existing foundation. For a wall like this, the first course of bricks would just be bedded on mortar and the bricks cut to fit.

CONSTRUCTING WALLS

Supporting piers and buttresses
If you are building a freestanding wall from scratch, over three courses high, it needs a foundation of compacted hardcore and a concrete slab, and piers about every 2 m. If it is two bricks thick, the piers are adequate, but if you want to cut costs and build a single-brick-thick wall, supporting buttresses will also be needed about every 1 m.

Corners and junctions
Corners and junctions are created by changing the direction of the bricks, arranging them in such a way that the corner or junction can be achieved without changing the bond. Right angles are the easiest to achieve.

Sloping sites
If the slope is gentle, dig a deep trench, lay a concrete slab below ground level, then build the

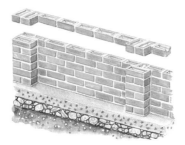

ABOVE A single-brick wall, with piers at regular intervals.

ABOVE A wall that runs up a slope needs a stepped foundation.

wall. But if the slope is extreme, dig the trench and construct a stepped concrete slab (all below ground), making the concrete risers the same thickness as a brick (see lower illustration).

Curved walls
If the curve is big enough, the bricks can be nudged slightly so that the vertical joints open up and allow the bricks to run around the curve. But if the curve is tight, the easiest option is to either use half-bricks – like building an arch – or to stand the bricks on edge and build the wall from soldier courses.

Coping
A coping functions like a hat – it throws rain away from the face of the wall and stops it soaking into the wall. It also has a decorative purpose – it is a way of finishing off the wall and making it pleasing to the eye.

OTHER STRUCTURES

Box structures
Plan the bond so that the bricks can be run from side to corner, and from corner to side, without being cut.

Arches
In garden brickwork, arches are best built either from half-bricks, or from bricks that run through the thickness of the wall. Either way, the bricks are placed so that the stretcher (side) or header (end) face of the brick is looking to the inside of the arch.

Columns and pillars
The simplest freestanding column or pillar can be merely a brick square, with the bricks turned 90° in neighbouring courses, and each course showing either a stretcher or a pair of headers (opposite left). However, the best option is to go for a pillar that has a stretcher alongside a header in every course (opposite right).

ABOVE Whole bricks running on their stretcher face.

LEFT A minimal, two-by-two pillar for rough work.

ABOVE A single-brick-thick wall with an arch made of half-bricks.

LEFT A four-by-four pillar for top-quality work.

Patios, paths and steps

Patios, paths and steps are an essential part of everyday life. If you need one of these structures for your garden, what better way of making it than by laying a pattern of bricks. Whether you are planning a minute patio outside the back door, a functional path running the length of the garden, or a very short decorative step up to the front door, bricks will do the job beautifully. Old bricks have a special character and charm.

CONSTRUCTING PATIOS AND PATHS

Patios

A patio always needs a foundation to stop it sinking, and an edging to stop it spreading. These need to be equal (in size, structure and permanence) to the composition of the soil, the character of the patio, the combined weight of the materials, and to the expected usage. A firm, dry, stony soil requires the minimum of groundwork, but a wet, soft site requires hardcore, concrete and drainage, plus an edging complete with a foundation.

Paths

Because a path gets heavier use than a patio, it needs a deeper foundation and a more permanent edging. The stucture of the edging might need to change over its length depending on the characteristics of the garden that borders it (e.g lawn, flowerbed).

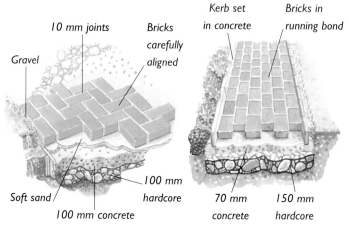

ABOVE **A patio foundation with formwork left in place.**

ABOVE **A path foundation with extra depth of hardcore.**

PATTERNS FOR PATIOS AND PATHS

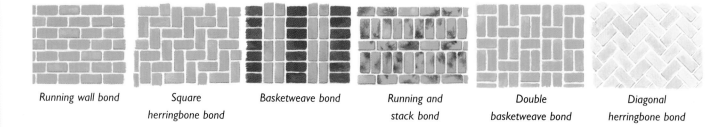

Running wall bond

Square
herringbone bond

Basketweave bond

Running and
stack bond

Double
basketweave bond

Diagonal
herringbone bond

CONSTRUCTING STEPS

Steps in the garden

The height (riser measurement) and width of a step are very important. Steps should be no greater than 230 mm high, and no less than 60 mm high (a good average would be 150 mm). The width of the tread should be at least 300–400 mm (front to back).

A single step on firm ground only needs a foundation of compacted hardcore. If the soil is soft and you want three or more steps, the bottom tread must be built on a firm foundation of 130 mm of compacted hardcore and 130 mm of concrete.

A doorstep gets a lot of use, and needs a firm foundation of 100 mm of compacted hardcore and 100 mm of concrete.

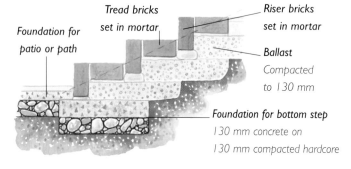

ABOVE **If you want to ensure that the structure is extra-firm, replicate the foundation for the bottom step under every step (do not use ballast).**

Finishing and maintenance

It doesn't take long to transform a pile of bricks, a heap of sand and lots of bags of cement into walls, paths, a patio and other brick structures – all of which need to be finished off and cleaned. Occasionally, the brickwork will also need maintenance. This section shows you how. Remember that by keeping bricks free from plant growth and filling in cavities, you will help prevent frost damage.

CLEANING BRICKWORK AFTER BUILDING

Basic cleaning

If you take care, when laying bricks, not to splash, squirt and smear mortar on the face of the brickwork, there should not be too much cleaning to do. Once the mortar has been allowed to dry overnight, use a stick of wood and a wire brush to knock off, and brush off, occasional splashes of mortar (concentrating on the brick and avoiding the mortar joints).

ABOVE Use a wire brush and work diagonally, so that you don't scour mortar out of the joints.

Chemical cleaning

Some types of brick can be cleaned with a special chemical that is sprayed or brushed on. This should only be used if recommended by the manufacturer of the bricks you are using, since it is possible to damage brickwork if used on the wrong type of brick.

Salts and efflorescence

A white powdery residue or "salting" may develop on the bricks, depending on type. This can be left, brushed off, or treated with vinegar or a chemical cleaner. On reconstituted stone (concrete products) such as block pavers or slabs, a patchy white effect may appear on the surface. This is normal and referred to as efflorescence. It is temporary but can be removed with special cleaners.

CLEANING: THINGS TO AVOID

- Do not touch mortar when it is still wet; leave overnight before cleaning.
- Do not let mortar become iron-hard before cleaning.
- Try not to wash away mortar from the joints.
- Do not scrape the surface of the bricks with metal tools.
- Avoid leaving a mortar residue when washing off the bricks.
- Do not use chemicals on brickwork unless recommended by the manufacturer.

MAINTAINING BRICKWORK

With brickwork projects, little or no maintenance is expected. Bricks should last several lifetimes; however, there are problems that may occur. Poor-quality bricks can crumble, frost can damage the surface of the bricks, or a brick may crack (cracks usually indicate poor pointing – see below for how to remedy). Mortar can be eroded quickly if the mortar mix was poorly measured out; erosion is also possible after many years, especially when exposed to lots of harsh, wet weather.

Repointing

Repointing is the process of replacing some of the mortar between the bricks, and is necessary when the original mortar has been eroded. Before adding slivers of new mortar, it may first be necessary to rake or chisel out mortar to make an adequate recess of 12–15 mm deep. Experiment with a small area first, in order to ensure a good colour match. Finish as you would for normal pointing (see page 27).

Replacing bricks

Find a new, matching brick, and use a bolster chisel and a club hammer to cut out the damaged brick. Avoid damaging the surrounding bricks by levering with the chisel. Chisel out all the mortar in the recess and brush out the dust. Dampen the bottom and sides of the hole a little, prior to lining with stiff mortar. Put mortar on top of the replacement brick and carefully push it in place. Finish the joints as normal (see page 27).

Reinforcing brickwork

If brickwork in your garden is showing signs of structural failure, you will have to repair it. If the top of a wall is disintegrating, the top few courses need to be relaid and a protective coping added.

If brickwork is cracked or leaning, the foundation is failing. If the problem doesn't look too bad, reinforce or underpin the foundation, bit by bit, with sections of additional concrete, and replace the damaged brickwork. If the wall looks really dreadful, demolish it.

Part 2: **Projects**

Flower border edging

If your flower borders merge into the lawn, smarten them up with a neat brick edging. This traditional English design, commonly found in Sussex, uses rows of beautiful handmade bricks to form a decorative edge that separates the earth from the lawn. It looks very attractive, especially in a cottage garden. Brick edging is also a wonderful timesaver when it comes to mowing the lawn.

TIME
One weekend per 5 m length of edging.

SPECIAL TIPS
This design is intended for straight borders, but it can also be used for gentle curves (experiment without mortar before you build).

CUT-AWAY DETAIL OF THE FLOWER BORDER EDGING

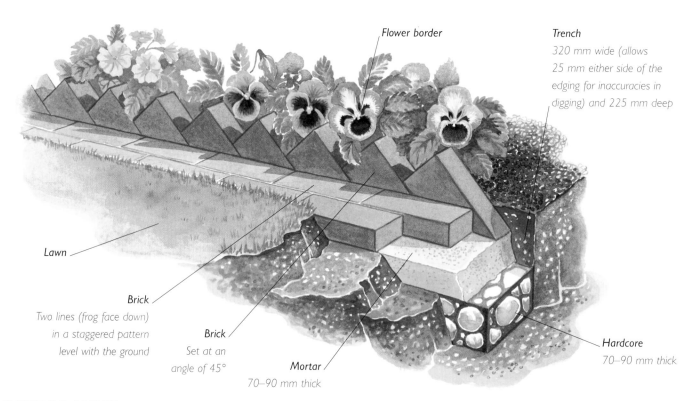

Flower border

Trench
320 mm wide (allows 25 mm either side of the edging for inaccuracies in digging) and 225 mm deep

Lawn

Brick
Two lines (frog face down) in a staggered pattern level with the ground

Brick
Set at an angle of 45°

Mortar
70–90 mm thick

Hardcore
70–90 mm thick

BORDER LINES

This design is very practical: the rows of bricks are laid at the same level as the lawn, making it easy to mow (and less work to trim). The lawnmower can be pushed hard up against the zigzag edging that holds back the earth, with its wheels running along the brick track next to it.

There are a number of options you may want to consider before starting. First of all, think about the style of your garden and whether or not this traditional English pattern is suitable. For a more modern look, for example, you could have a single line of black bricks partnered with a line of blue glazed tiles.

This is a very simple project to make and you are unlikely to encounter any problems. In fact, it is an ideal project to begin with if you are new to brickwork.

YOU WILL NEED

Materials *for an edging 5 m long and 270 mm wide*
• Bricks: 85
• Hardcore: 0.2 cu. metres
• Mortar: 1 part (36 kg) cement and 4 parts (144 kg) sand

Tools
• Tape measure, pegs and string
• Spade and fork
• Wheelbarrow and bucket
• Sledgehammer
• Shovel and mixing board, or cement mixer
• Bricklayer's trowel
• Club hammer
• Bolster chisel

Step-by-step: Making the flower border edging

Digging
Dig out the earth in shallow spadefuls

Turf
Remove the turf first and see if it can be used elsewhere in the garden

String
Make sure that the two strings remain taut and parallel

1 Decide where to put the edging (we wanted to increase the width of an existing flower border and avoid damaging plants). Use the pegs and string to mark an area 320 mm wide (this allows 25 mm either side of the edging for inaccuracies in digging) and as long as your border. Use the spade and fork to remove the turf and dig a trench 225 mm deep. Remove the pegs and string.

Hardcore
Systematically break and compact the hardcore until you have a level layer

2 Spread hardcore in the trench and use the sledgehammer to compact it. Break up any pieces larger than half a brick. Continue spreading hardcore, breaking and compacting until you have filled the trench with 70–90 mm of hardcore. Remove any pieces that stick up above this height.

Club hammer
Allow the weight of the
hammer to do the work

Flower border
Remove the
turf to
extend the
border when
the edging is
in place

3 Spread mortar along a
1 m-long section of trench,
using the bricklayer's trowel,
making it 70–90 mm thick. Don't
try to do more than 1 m at a
time. Position two lines of bricks
(frog face down) in a staggered
pattern and knock them level
with the ground using the handle
of the club hammer. Use the club
hammer and bolster chisel to cut
half-bricks when needed.

Level
Try to keep the
bricks level with
each other
(and slightly
lower than
the level of
the lawn)

Guide
Use the width
of a brick
to ascertain
the depth of
the zigzag

4 Position the angled bricks
carefully and tap them into
the bed of mortar. Aim for an
angle of 45°. You can use another
brick as a guide to how far the
brick needs to sink down (as
shown); alternatively just knock it
in so that it appears even. Finish
the section; repeat the procedure
to complete the edging.

Helpful hint

After placing about six
angled bricks, stand back
and check that they are all
at 45° and pushed down to
the correct depth. If things
go wrong, just pull out the
offending bricks, add extra
mortar and replace them in
the correct position.

Country cottage path

One of the best ways of creating a joyous splash of colour and pattern in the garden is to build a red brick path in the country cottage tradition. It's a beautifully simple concept that involves gathering as many bricks as you can find – the older and more battered the better – and arranging them in a three-by-three basketweave pattern.

YOU WILL NEED

Materials *for a path 4 m long and 690 mm wide*
- Bricks: 186
- Hardcore: 0.25 cu. metres
- Ballast: 250 kg
- Sand: 250 kg
- Mortar: 1 part (15 kg) cement and 4 parts (60 kg) sand
- Wood: 8 m of 80 x 40 mm section (formwork), 6 pieces (minimum), 300 mm long, 35 mm wide and 20 mm thick (pegs), 1 piece, 690 mm long, 115 mm wide and 20 mm thick; 1 piece, 795 mm long, 35 mm wide and 20 mm thick (screeding board)
- Nails: 6 (minimum) x 50 mm (formwork), and 2 x 35 mm (screeding board)

Tools
- Tape measure, pegs and string
- Club hammer
- Spade and fork
- Wheelbarrow and bucket
- Sledgehammer
- General-purpose saw
- Claw hammer
- Plate compacter
- Shovel and mixing board, or cement mixer
- Bricklayer's trowel
- Rake
- Broom

PAVING THE WAY

Many beautiful gardens feature patterned brickwork paths. The warm tones of clay bricks arranged in small-scale, intricate patterns look wonderful, especially on a hazy summer's day when they are set against the fresh tones of foliage and a bright patchwork of flowers.

Various combinations of brick colour and layout pattern allow endless design possibilities. This basketweave design will look great in traditional, cottage-type gardens. Most designs entail the same building techniques as this path. The path is ideal for light use and is just the right width to permit a wheelbarrow to be pushed along it. If you need a wider path, let the pattern of bricks dictate the precise width (and avoid cutting bricks as much as possible).

You won't be digging down too deep to make the foundation, so do not worry about exposing pipes leading to and from the house; however, take the usual precautions when siting the path. Check the location of underground utility pipes (gas, water main, drains, oil supplies) and avoid situating a project nearby.

CUT-AWAY DETAIL OF THE COUNTRY COTTAGE PATH

Pegs
Nailed to formwork

Formwork
Set level with the ground

Brick edging
Line of bricks set in mortar to be level with formwork

Mortar

Dug-out area
795 mm wide and 248 mm deep

Basketweave pattern

Additional sand
Added to maintain a recess 110 mm deep

Sand
15 mm thick

Ballast
35 mm thick

Hardcore
75 mm thick

Step-by-step: **Making the country cottage path**

Hardcore
Pound into small pieces
to form a compact layer

Screeding board
Use the board to spread
and level the ballast

Sledgehammer
Choose a
hammer weight
to suit your
strength

Path width
The space
between the
formwork
boards should
be 690 mm

Pegs
Fixed to
outer side of
formwork

1 Plan where the path is to go and use the tape measure, club hammer, pegs and string to mark out an area on the ground 795 mm wide and as long as required. Dig out the turf and soil to a depth of 248 mm using the spade and fork. Spread hardcore in the trench and pound it with a sledgehammer to break up large pieces and form a compacted, level layer 75 mm thick.

2 Nail pegs to the outer side of the formwork and position it in the trench so that it is level with the ground on either side. Test that your bricks fit within the formwork by laying out a small area of pattern. Spread ballast to just above the level of the bottom of the formwork and use the plate compacter to compact it into a layer 35 mm thick. Make a screeding board and scrape away the excess ballast.

3 Mix up some stiff mortar and lay a line of bricks either side of the path, setting them on their stretcher face (side). Do not leave gaps between the bricks. Tap them level with the top of the formwork and use the trowel to scrape away the excess mortar that squeezes out from under the bricks.

Mortar
Scrape away
excess mortar

Edging
Set the bricks
level with the
formwork

Working action
Use a gentle tapping
and dragging action

Screeding
board
Revise the size
of the board to
allow for the
15 mm of
sand that has
been added

4 Once the mortar has set, spread a layer of sand and use the plate compacter to compact it into a layer 15 mm thick. Avoid vibrating and dislodging the edge bricks. Spread more sand and revise the size of the screeding board so that it fits between the rows of edge bricks. Scrape away excess sand to leave a recess, approximately 110 mm deep, for the rest of the bricks.

Depth
Check the
depth of the
recess – it
needs to be
110 mm

Size and colour
Experiment
to find the
most attractive
arrangement
of colours and
the best fit

5 Lay the bricks, stretcher face up, in the basketweave pattern. Avoid treading on the sand. Work from one end to the other and occasionally stand back to check your progress. When all the bricks have been laid, brush sand into the joints. Fix a pad (or piece of carpet) to the plate compacter and run it over the bricks.

Helpful hint

Because bricks are proportioned to allow for the mortar joints used in bricklaying, the gaps between the bricks at the sides and ends will vary. Compensate for this by distributing them as evenly as possible.

Raised herringbone patio

The wonderful thing about a patio is that it immediately becomes a focal point, and broadens the way you use the garden. It makes a great surface for a barbecue, the perfect place for a family meal, and a super-safe area for children to play on. If you enjoy doing puzzles, you will like the process of laying the herringbone surface.

TIME

Three days to prepare the foundation and one day to complete the patio.

SPECIAL TIPS

A raised patio requires less digging and earth removal than a ground-level patio.

CUT-AWAY DETAIL OF THE RAISED HERRINGBONE PATIO

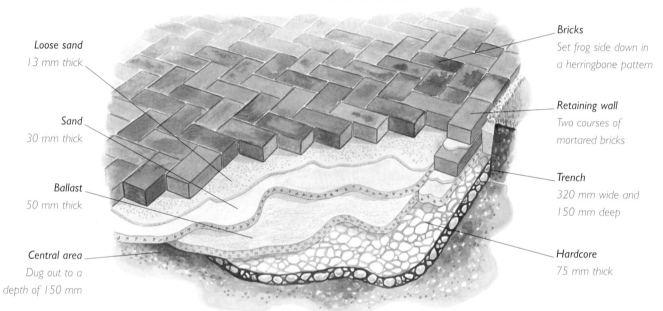

Loose sand
13 mm thick

Sand
30 mm thick

Ballast
50 mm thick

Central area
Dug out to a
depth of 150 mm

Bricks
Set frog side down in
a herringbone pattern

Retaining wall
Two courses of
mortared bricks

Trench
320 mm wide and
150 mm deep

Hardcore
75 mm thick

YOU WILL NEED

Materials *for a patio*
3.024 m square
- Bricks: 104 (retaining wall) and 351 (patio surface)
- Hardcore: 0.75 cu. metres
- Ballast: 1 tonne
- Sand: 1 tonne
- Mortar: 1 part (20 kg) cement and 4 parts (80 kg) sand
- Wood: 1 piece, 3 m long, 150 mm wide and 20 mm thick (screeding board)

Tools
- Tape measure, pegs and string
- Club hammer
- Spade and fork
- Wheelbarrow and bucket
- Sledgehammer
- Shovel and mixing board, or cement mixer
- Bricklayer's trowel and pointing trowel
- Spirit level
- Plate compacter
- Rake
- Bolster chisel
- Broom

A PATTERN TO FOLLOW

If you have a small, modern courtyard, you can adjust this design to make it less quaint – perhaps by inserting contrasting zigzags of stone, inlaid wood or textured metal. Or a variation in the pattern might appeal (see pages 28 and 30), but bear in mind that some patterns require many more bricks to be cut and therefore it will take longer to make the patio.

This concept of a raised patio built within a retaining wall is often chosen in order to minimize the building work involved in a patio project, because less earth needs digging and removing from the site than for a ground-level patio. Even so, remember that building any patio is hard work, and fairly costly because you are usually dealing with a large area. Save up for quality bricks, allocate a few weekends to complete the work, and enlist some help.

When surveying your site, consider the finished height of the patio in relation to existing doorways, steps or paths. If the patio is to be attached to the house, do not cover air bricks (perforated bricks near the bottom of the walls of the house) and do not build the patio any higher than 150 mm below the damp course of the house. Most importantly, the patio should slope away from the house by 25 mm per 2 m.

Step-by-step: **Making the raised herringbone patio**

Trench
Dig out to 320 mm
wide and 150 mm deep

1 Using the tape measure, pegs, string and club hammer, mark out the size and position of the patio, allowing an extra 100 mm all around (3.232 m square). If you are building against a wall, do not add on an extra 100 mm on that side. Check that the patio area is square (see page 21). Dig a trench (320 mm wide and 150 mm deep) all around the edge, within the square. Spread hardcore in the trench and compact with the sledgehammer to a finished depth of 75 mm.

Hardcore
Compact the hardcore until it is level and 75 mm thick

Level
Remove stubborn pieces that stand proud

2 Build a two-brick-high retaining wall along the middle of the trench. Lay the first course of bricks on a generous thickness of mortar, leaving 10 mm-wide joints between the bricks. Check that the wall is straight and level (or sloping away from your house as appropriate). Finish the joints with the pointing trowel (by inserting mortar if necessary, smoothing, scraping away and creating a slight dip between the edges of adjoining bricks). Lay the second course with the frog face downwards.

Club hammer
Use the handle of the hammer to knock the bricks into position

Wall
Build the wall two bricks high. On the top course, lay the frog face downwards

Wall
Top course of the wall
forms the edging

Plate
compacter
A safe, easy-
to-use machine

3 While you are waiting for the mortar to set, dig out the central area within the wall to a depth of 150 mm. Spread a layer of hardcore and using the sledgehammer, break and compact it to a depth of 75 mm. Spread a thick layer of ballast and compact it with the plate compacter until 50 mm deep, followed by a layer of sand compacted to a depth of 30 mm. Prepare a 3 m-long screeding board by cutting a 65 mm (brick height) x 115 mm notch out of both ends. Ask someone to hold the other end and scrape off excess sand by dragging the board across the patio area whilst the notched ends are engaged with the brick wall.

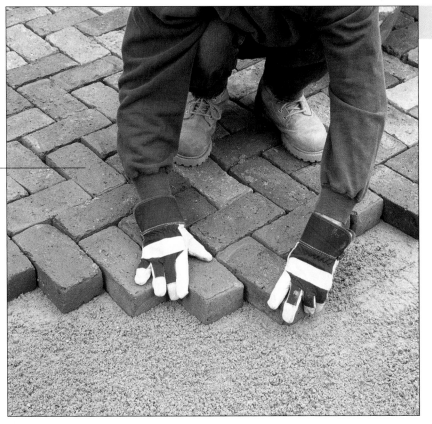

Bricks
Arrange bricks
(frog side
down) for
best fit and
colour effect

4 Fill low areas with more sand and compact again. Screed once more and then rake 13 mm of loose sand over the whole area. Lay the bricks in a herringbone pattern. Using the bolster chisel and club hammer, cut bricks to fill the small gaps. Sweep sand into the joints. Fix a pad (or piece of carpet) to the plate compacter and run the machine over the bricks.

Helpful hint

Aim for even gaps between the bricks; stand back every now and then to check your progress. For areas larger than 3 m square, use a string line as a guide to laying the bricks in a straight line.

Classic birdbath

A birdbath must surely be one of the most decorative and interesting things to have in a garden. If you enjoy watching birds splashing the hours away, try building this straightforward pillar, which is topped with a ready-made birdbath. Site it so that it can be viewed from a patio, or the house, for year-round entertainment value.

TIME

Half a day to make the foundation and four days to build the pillar.

SPECIAL TIPS

This structure can also be used for mounting a sundial.

YOU WILL NEED

Materials *for a pillar 1.09 m high and 553 mm square*
- Bricks: 82
- Tiles: 36 tiles, 143 mm square and 8 mm thick
- Paving slab: 440 mm square and 35 mm thick
- Hardcore: 0.1 cu. metres
- Concrete: 1 part (40 kg) cement and 4 parts (160 kg) ballast
- Mortar: 1 part (12 kg) cement and 4 parts (48 kg) sand
- Wood: 4 pieces, 690 mm long, 120 mm wide and 40 mm thick (formwork), 4 pieces, 393 mm long, 75 mm wide and 47 mm thick (collar)
- Nails: 16 x 80 mm
- Birdbath dish: 345 mm square and 84 mm high

Tools
- Tape measure and piece of chalk
- General-purpose saw
- Claw hammer
- Spade
- Wheelbarrow and bucket
- Sledgehammer
- Spirit level
- Shovel and mixing board, or cement mixer
- Bricklayer's trowel and pointing trowel
- Bolster chisel
- Rubber mallet
- Tile cutter

A FASCINATING VIEW

Most of us enjoy watching birds in the garden, and a birdbath will help to attract them. This restrained, architectural-looking design also has other possibilities. Without the birdbath on top, the pillar can make a dramatic plinth for a classical statuette. (Fix the statue to the top with a 300 mm-long steel rod 10 mm in diameter. Drill a hole in the top of the pillar (10 mm in diameter) with a masonry bit, making it at least 150 mm deep. Drill a 150 mm-deep hole in the statue. Drop the rod into the pillar and put the statue on top. The rod will stop the statue being blown off or knocked off.) The pillar could also form the base for a sundial.

Personalize the design by choosing a birdbath handmade from metal, stone or wood, or a decorative shallow ceramic pot. The tile details could also be altered – perhaps a line of tiles on every course, or thick black slate substituted instead. Decorative patterned tiles could also be inserted into the brickwork.

EXPLODED VIEW OF THE CLASSIC BIRDBATH

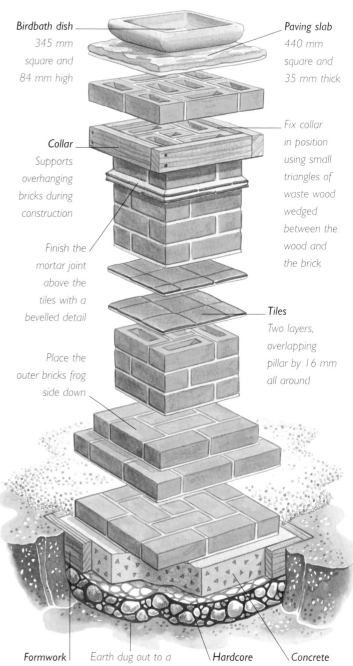

Birdbath dish
345 mm square and 84 mm high

Paving slab
440 mm square and 35 mm thick

Collar
Supports overhanging bricks during construction

Fix collar in position using small triangles of waste wood wedged between the wood and the brick

Finish the mortar joint above the tiles with a bevelled detail

Tiles
Two layers, overlapping pillar by 16 mm all around

Place the outer bricks frog side down

Formwork frame

Earth dug out to a depth of 300 mm

Hardcore 180 mm

Concrete 120 mm

Step-by-step: **Making the classic birdbath**

Edging bricks
Place these bricks with the frog face downwards

Centre bricks
Arrange the inner bricks with frog face uppermost

I Make the formwork frame using two 80 mm nails at each corner. Lay the frame on the ground and roughly mark around it with the spade. Put the frame aside and dig out the marked earth to a depth of 300 mm. Fill the area with hardcore and compact it to a thickness of 180 mm with the sledgehammer. Lay the frame on top and make sure that it is level, then fill with concrete. When the concrete is dry, practise laying the first course of bricks.

Rubber mallet
Using this avoids damaging the bricks

Third course
Bricks placed frog face down

Joints
Note the staggered arrangement of the vertical joints

Level
Make sure all the bricks are bedded to the same level. Note that the outer bricks are used frog side down

Pointing
Use the pointing trowel to point the joints

2 Chalk around the bricks. Remove them and spread mortar within the marks. Lay the first course and ensure that it is level and square by checking the side and diagonal measurements (see page 21). Lay the second course in the same way, but with the vertical joints staggered.

3 Clean up the joints of the first two courses. Practise laying the third course, which is stepped inwards. Mark its position with chalk, and lay the bricks on a bed of mortar. Repeat for the fourth course. Continue building up to the level of the tiles and leave the pillar overnight.

Levelling
Sandwich and bed the tiles
in mortar and tap level

Tiles
Cut and fit the
tiles so that
they overhang
by 16 mm

Mortar
Rake out
a little of
the mortar
between
the tiles

4 Cut and fit two layers of tiles to cover the area, allowing an overlap of 16 mm all around the pillar. Make sure that none of the joints coincide. The tiles can be quite tricky to lay neatly, so work slowly and carefully. Use the spirit level to check that they are level.

Wooden collar
Make a frame
that fits loosely
around the top
of the pillar and
wedge it in
place with small
triangles of
waste wood so
that it cannot
move. The collar
will support the
weight of the
overhanging
bricks. (When
the project is
complete, wait
48 hours
before removing
the collar)

5 Continue building up the courses of brick and tile that create the pillar, checking that each course is level and the corners remain vertical. Make the wooden collar to support the final overhanging layer of bricks and wedge it in place. Build the final course of bricks. Position the slab and clean up the joints. Place the birdbath dish on top.

Helpful hint

Positioning the collar is difficult to do on your own, so ask somebody to help. If the collar keeps slipping down or going crooked, try using differently shaped wedges, and more of them.

Planted patio

Just imagine a warm summer's evening, when you can sit outside enjoying the stored

heat given off by the patio, and wafts of scent from surrounding plants. This patio

design incorporates beds of earth, which have been planted with a selection of herbs.

Concrete paving blocks, bricks or clay paving blocks can be used for the paving.

TIME

Five days to prepare the
foundation and two days
to lay the blocks.

SPECIAL TIPS

If you want a different
pattern of blocks,
experiment by arranging
them on the ground.

YOU WILL NEED

Materials *for a planted patio 4.815 m square*
- Concrete paving blocks: 714 blocks, 200 mm long, 100 mm wide and 50 mm thick (or bricks or clay paving blocks – if using these, adjust quantity, overall patio measurements and depth of foundation)
- Hardcore: 2.5 cu. metres
- Concrete: 1 part (500 kg) cement and 4 parts (2 tonnes) ballast
- Mortar: 1 part (75 kg) cement and 4 parts (300 kg) sand
- Wood: 28 m of 150 x 22 mm section (formwork), 56 pieces, 300 mm long, 35 mm wide and 22 mm thick (formwork pegs),

and 1 piece, 1.6 m long, 100 mm wide and 22 mm thick (tamping board)
- Nails: 172 x 38 mm

Tools
- Tape measure, pegs and string
- Spade and fork
- Wheelbarrow and bucket
- General-purpose saw
- Claw hammer
- Spirit level
- Club hammer
- Sledgehammer
- Shovel and mixing board, or cement mixer
- Bolster chisel
- Pointing trowel
- Gardener's trowel

SETTING THE STYLE

This design offers a blend of planting and paving reminiscent of a medieval herb garden. It can be enjoyed as a pathway through a miniature landscape, or somewhere to sit in peace on your own, or as a place to savour the fragrance of herbs. If you wish, you can change the balance of planting to paving, or move the planting to one side and have a larger paved area for sitting.

Patios require a big investment in time and materials, so make sure that you can manage a project of this size. You shouldn't come across any pipes whilst digging the foundation, because it isn't very deep, but always be cautious and get advice if you uncover pipes that you were not expecting. The major part of the work is the digging and the setting out of the wooden formwork, so don't be dismayed if things seem slow at first.

CUT-AWAY VIEW OF
THE PLANTED PATIO

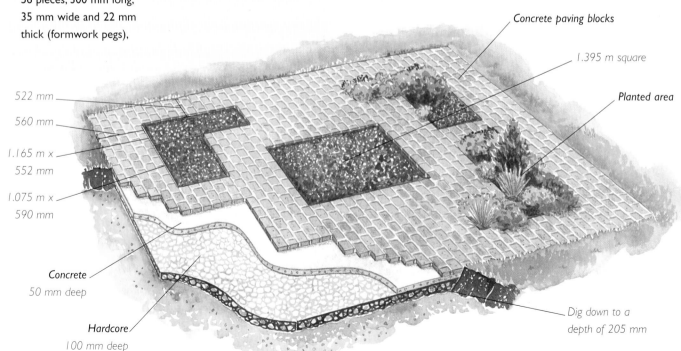

Concrete paving blocks

1.395 m square

Planted area

522 mm

560 mm

1.165 m x
552 mm

1.075 m x
590 mm

Concrete
50 mm deep

Hardcore
100 mm deep

Dig down to a
depth of 205 mm

Step-by-step: **Making the planted patio**

Hardcore
Compact to a depth of 100 mm and
30–40 mm lower than the formwork

Formwork
Build formwork
frames using
two nails at
each corner.
Nail pegs to
the inside of
the frames

| Dig out a level area of earth 4.815 m square and 205 mm deep. Mark out the paved and planted areas with pegs and string. Make up formwork frames to the size and shape of the planting areas. Knock these into the ground so that they are level with each other. Spread hardcore where the paving will be, and compact it to a depth of 100 mm.

Helpful hint

You will get a slightly better result if you can leave a gap between the hardcore and the formwork. With this method, the concrete will form a stronger edge around the planting areas.

Concrete
Should have a
crumbly texture

2 Mix up some concrete using very little water (it should be crumbly), and shovel it over the hardcore. Use the tamping board to tamp the concrete level with the top of the formwork. It is possible to work on your own, but the task is much easier if you have help. Either way, do not tread on the concrete, and do not try to build more than a quarter of the patio in one go.

Tamping
Tamp the
concrete level
with the top of
the formwork

Bedding
Dampen the underside of the
bricks and wiggle into place

String line
Use a taut
string line as
a guide

 3 Without waiting for the concrete to dry, set up a string line to indicate where to lay the first line of blocks and gently bed each block, leaving gaps of about 15 mm between them. The concrete is already level, so there is no need to tap the blocks down or check levels – just wiggle them into position and occasionally stand back to check your lines are straight and gaps are equal.

Joints
Aim for joints
that are about
15 mm wide

Mortar
Push crumbly mortar
into the joints

Formwork
Remove the formwork
and fill with earth

Pointing
Use the handle
of the pointing
trowel to
smooth and
finish the joints

Plants
Choose plants
carefully. Before
planting, lay
them out in
their pots to
look at the
pattern you are
creating. Take
into account
their size when
fully grown.

Earth
Use a planting
mixture to suit
your plants

4 Use a bolster chisel and club hammer to cut blocks to fill in small spaces. Mix up some mortar using very little water (like the concrete, it should be crumbly) and scrape this into the gaps. Push it down into the gaps until you have filled the full depth. Finish the joints.

5 Leave the concrete and mortar to set fully (or wait at least two days) and then clean up any excess mortar. Remove the formwork, loosen the earth in the planting areas with the fork, and top them up with good soil or compost to the level of the bricks.

Inspirations: Brick patios

While patios made from concrete, reconstituted stone slabs or tarmac can be overpowering and visually intrusive, brick patios somehow seem to blend into their surroundings much better. A well-built brick patio looks charming, solid and imposing – perfect for just about everything from a cottage to a townhouse. The bricks can be laid in all sorts of patterns to create attractive designs, possibly incorporating different-coloured bricks or other materials.

ABOVE **A patio made from local bricks, seashore cobbles and field flints. The owner wanted to create an unexpected retreat in** a secluded part of the garden, and chose a semicircle outlined by pebbles to create an unusual, decorative shape.

ABOVE This sizeable stone and brick patio forms a practical and attractive surface around a farmhouse. The brickwork infill echoes the walls of the house, ensuring that the house and patio complement each other.

LEFT A huge brick patio that encircles a low dwarf hedge and looks rather like a very wide path. The patio is built to accommodate a sloping site – the outer edge is raised and the inner edge is flush with the turf by the hedge.

Decorative raised bed

Raised beds are a good idea: not only do they give you the chance to increase the planting area in your garden, but better still – especially if you find it difficult to bend – they bring the garden up to a more manageable height and make it very easy to tend the plants. A raised bed can make a very suitable home for rockery plants, enabling you to enjoy these miniature plants at close quarters.

TIME

One weekend
(longer if you need to build a foundation).

SPECIAL TIPS

You may need to use an angle grinder, which requires safety precautions (see pages 14 and 25).

CROSS-SECTION OF THE DECORATIVE RAISED BED

Coping tile
290 x 132 x 26 mm

Decorative tile
215 x 215 x 28 mm

Foundation
You may be able to use an existing area of paving as a foundation

Concrete
50 mm thick

Hardcore
100 mm thick

Additional bricks
Behind decorative tile

Planting mixture
Soil and compost

Drainage
Broken brick and pebbles to improve drainage

YOU WILL NEED

Materials *for a raised bed 1.148 m x 1.148 m minus square section to create L-shape, and 560 mm high*
- Bricks: 128
- Decorative tiles: 2 tiles, 215 mm square and 28 mm thick
- Coping tiles: 14 tiles, 290 mm long, 132 mm wide and 26 mm thick
- Mortar: 1 part (15 kg) cement and 4 parts (60 kg) sand

Tools
- Tape measure, straight-edge about 1.2 m long, and a piece of chalk
- Shovel and mixing board, or cement mixer
- Bricklayer's trowel and pointing trowel
- Spirit level
- Mason's hammer
- Bolster chisel
- Club hammer
- Angle grinder (may be required to cut the coping tiles)

RAISING THE STANDARDS

As with most projects, there are options and variations you might prefer instead of building exactly to the given specifications. If you are thinking about altering the size, remember that the size and shape of the bed both need careful consideration – it is tempting to build a bigger structure, but there is a danger of creating something that requires a massive amount of earth. This narrow corner design is great for small plants and doesn't need tonnes of soil to fill it. The decorative tiles make the building procedure more complicated, but are worth the extra trouble.

If you want to change the appearance of the raised bed, don't settle for boring materials until you have scoured the salvage yards for great-looking terracotta details or old-style patterned tiles. Brightly coloured Victorian glazed tiles with floral designs will look wonderful set against the warm colours of the brick. You may also want to consider using contrasting colours of brick in lines or patterns, as used in the Storage Seat project on page 68.

Decorative raised bed

PLAN VIEW SHOWING THE FIRST COURSE OF BRICKS

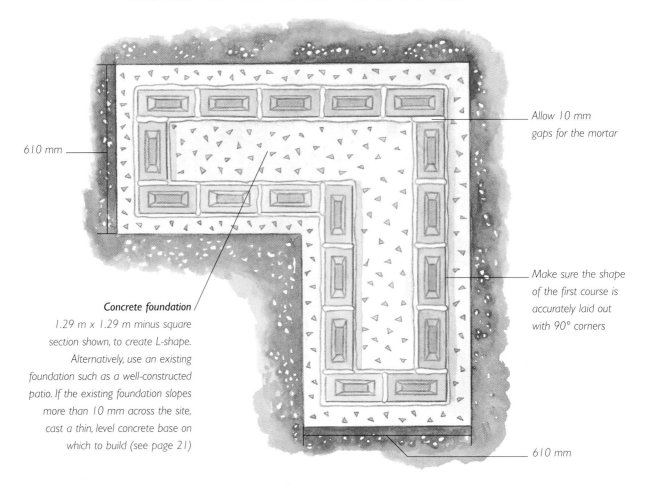

*Allow 10 mm
gaps for the mortar*

610 mm

Concrete foundation
*1.29 m x 1.29 m minus square
section shown, to create L-shape.
Alternatively, use an existing
foundation such as a well-constructed
patio. If the existing foundation slopes
more than 10 mm across the site,
cast a thin, level concrete base on
which to build (see page 21)*

*Make sure the shape
of the first course is
accurately laid out
with 90° corners*

610 mm

DETAIL SHOWING THE RECESS FOR THE DECORATIVE TILE

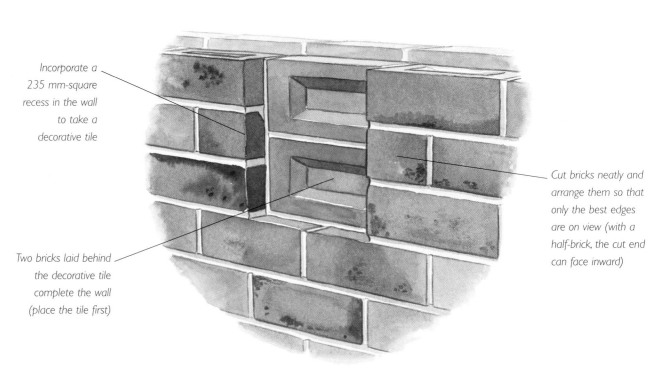

*Incorporate a
235 mm-square
recess in the wall
to take a
decorative tile*

*Two bricks laid behind
the decorative tile
complete the wall
(place the tile first)*

*Cut bricks neatly and
arrange them so that
only the best edges
are on view (with a
half-brick, the cut end
can face inward)*

EXPLODED VIEW OF THE DECORATIVE RAISED BED

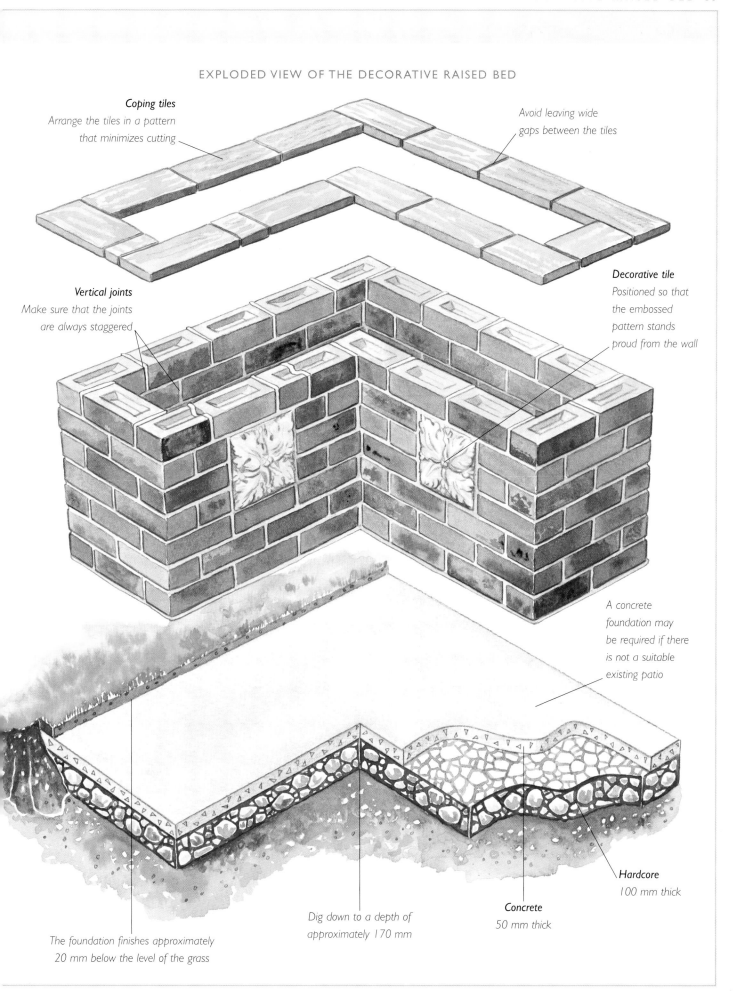

Coping tiles
Arrange the tiles in a pattern
that minimizes cutting

Avoid leaving wide
gaps between the tiles

Vertical joints
Make sure that the joints
are always staggered

Decorative tile
Positioned so that
the embossed
pattern stands
proud from the wall

A concrete
foundation may
be required if there
is not a suitable
existing patio

Hardcore
100 mm thick

Concrete
50 mm thick

Dig down to a depth of
approximately 170 mm

The foundation finishes approximately
20 mm below the level of the grass

Step-by-step: **Making the decorative raised bed**

First course
Arrange the bricks in the correct position, leaving 10 mm gaps in between

Marking out
Use a piece of chalk and a straight-edge to mark out the shape

1 Work out where you would like the bed. We have put it on the corner of a patio that has a foundation sufficiently adequate to support the additional weight of a raised bed. See pages 20–21 if you need to build a foundation. Practise arranging the first course of bricks to establish the size and shape of the bed, and use the tape measure, chalk and straight-edge to mark around them.

Corners
Check that the bricks form 90° corners

Levelling
Use the spirit level to help position the bricks accurately

Straight sides
Check that the bricks are in straight lines using the edge of the spirit level

2 Lay the first course of bricks on a bed of mortar. Use the spirit level to check that the bricks are accurately placed and stand back to scrutinise your work. The overall shape should have 90° corners, the sides should be straight, and the gaps between the bricks should be equal.

Pointing
Use the pointing trowel to scrape away the excess mortar and smooth the joints between the bricks

3 Lay a further two courses, making sure that each one is level and the vertical joints occur in the correct staggered positions. Clean up the joints using the pointing trowel.

Joints inside wall
Don't worry too much about the appearance of the mortar joints inside the structure – just scrape out the excess

Bricks
Use two bricks to weigh down the piece
of wood that holds the tile in place

Decorative tile
Check that it
is positioned
centrally and
vertically within
the space,
and that the
pattern stands
proud of
the bricks

4 Build the next three courses, leaving square spaces in the front-facing walls to receive the decorative tiles. Spread mortar in these spaces and position the tiles. Hold each tile in position by placing a piece of wood across the top of the walls and weighting it with a couple of bricks. Put bricks behind the tile to support it (see hint).

Helpful hint

Wait for the mortar fixing the bricks to dry, stack bricks inside the space behind the tile, and use a wooden prop to push the tile against the pile of bricks.

Spirit level
Use the edge
of the spirit
level to help
you position
the coping
tiles in a
straight line

5 Complete the last course of bricks. Note how the bricks in this course are cut (using the mason's hammer) and arranged so that the joints do not coincide with the edges of the tile below (see main picture). Practise arranging the coping tiles in a pattern that minimizes cutting. Use the bolster chisel and club hammer, or angle grinder, to cut tiles. Bed the coping tiles on 10 mm of mortar, using the side of the spirit level to help align the edges of the tiles.

Simple garden wall

There is something very enjoyable about building a simple brick wall – the process of trowelling slices of soft, smooth mortar, and placing one brick upon another, is a great escape from everyday worries. This freestanding low wall is suitable for a front garden wall, a wall around a raised patio, or a retaining wall for a small flower border. Or perhaps you have a unstable wall with missing bricks, which needs replacing.

TIME
Three days for a 3 m length of wall.

SAFETY
If you want a bigger wall, see page 29 for details on wall size and safety.

CROSS-SECTION DETAIL OF THE SIMPLE GARDEN WALL

Coping bricks

Bricks
Laid in normal stretcher bond

Concrete
90 mm thick

Hardcore
90 mm thick

Tiles
Two layers of decorative tiles help the wall shed rainwater

Soldier bricks
Headers (ends) facing forwards

You may be able to use an existing foundation such as a strongly built patio

YOU WILL NEED

Materials *for a wall 3 m long and 518 mm high*
- Bricks: 180
- Tiles: 36 tiles, 265 mm long, 175 mm wide and 10 mm thick
- Mortar: 1 part (25 kg) cement and 4 parts (100 kg) sand
- Wood: 1 piece, 3 m long, 100 mm wide and 22 mm thick (levelling board)

Tools
- Shovel and mixing board, or cement mixer
- Wheelbarrow and bucket
- Bricklayer's trowel and pointing trowel
- Spirit level
- Mason's hammer

THE GREAT DIVIDE

A two-brick-thick wall is a good choice for most garden walls and will look better and last longer than the single-brick alternative. The pattern of bricks used in this wall is a traditional arrangement, and the layers of protruding tiles and bevelled mortar detail are not just for decoration – to some extent they also protect the structure from water erosion. If you are contemplating a higher wall, you will need extra support (see page 29 on Supporting Piers and Buttresses) and you would certainly need a more substantial foundation. For a wall that is twice as high, increase the size of the concrete foundation slab to three times the width of the wall, and increase the thickness of the slab by 30 mm. A beginner should not attempt to build a wall higher than about 2 m.

This low wall is built on an existing foundation (see page 21 for how to assess suitability). See page 29 for how to build curved walls, change angles and build around corners.

Simple garden wall

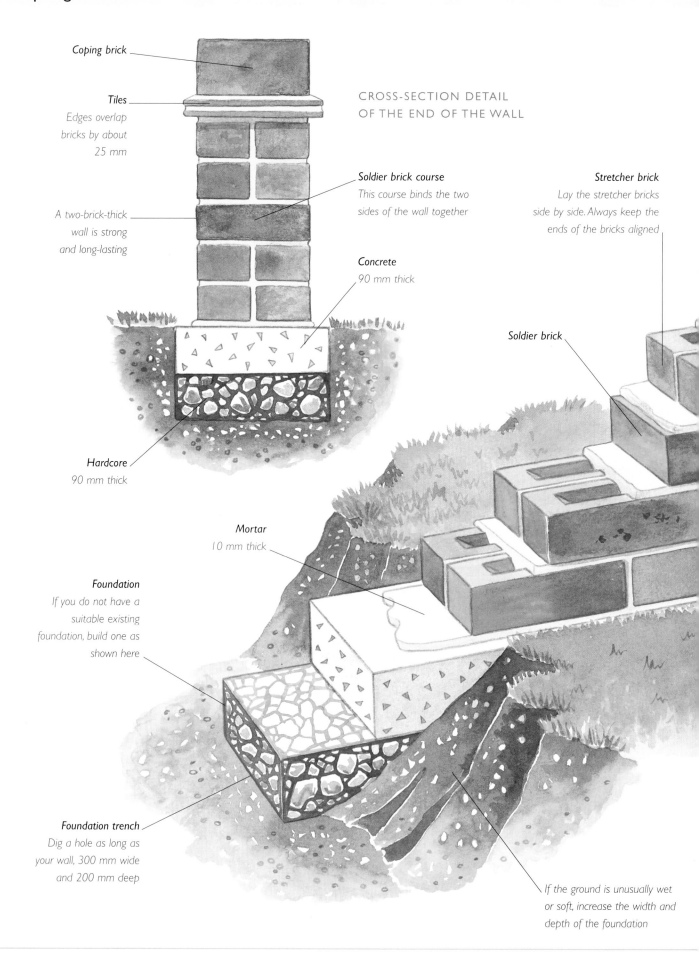

Coping brick

Tiles
*Edges overlap
bricks by about
25 mm*

CROSS-SECTION DETAIL
OF THE END OF THE WALL

*A two-brick-thick
wall is strong
and long-lasting*

Soldier brick course
*This course binds the two
sides of the wall together*

Stretcher brick
*Lay the stretcher bricks
side by side. Always keep the
ends of the bricks aligned*

Concrete
90 mm thick

Soldier brick

Hardcore
90 mm thick

Mortar
10 mm thick

Foundation
*If you do not have a
suitable existing
foundation, build one as
shown here*

Foundation trench
*Dig a hole as long as
your wall, 300 mm wide
and 200 mm deep*

*If the ground is unusually wet
or soft, increase the width and
depth of the foundation*

CUT-AWAY DETAIL OF THE SIMPLE GARDEN WALL

Coping brick

Tile

*Arrange the tiles so that
the joints are staggered*

DETAIL OF THE MORTAR
JOINT AROUND THE TILES

Coping brick

Mortar
10 mm thick

Sloped mortar

*Shape and smooth the mortar to make
a sloped surface, triangular in section*

Tile

*If the tiles are slightly curved, lay
them so that the convex (dished)
surfaces face each other*

Step-by-step: Making the simple garden wall

First course
Bed pairs of
bricks on mortar

Levelling
Use the levelling board
and spirit level

Foundation
In this instance,
there is a good,
solid foundation
under the patio

Bond
Build two
courses of
stretcher bond

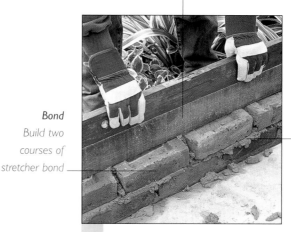

Cleaning up
Wait until the
mortar has
partly dried,
then clean
it up

1 If there is a suitable foundation (see page 21), you can start laying the bricks. Lay the first course of bricks on a generous bed of mortar. The bricks in each row should be equally spaced (10 mm joints) and placed exactly opposite each other. Check that the bricks are level and make adjustments as necessary.

2 Continue building the wall, this time staggering the joints of the second course so that they occur halfway along the bricks of the first course. Check the course is horizontal using the levelling board and the spirit level. (At this point, you could also use a line set to help you, which establishes a level and a straight line, and is usually employed in the construction of long walls and houses – see page 12.)

Aligning
Use the handle
of the hammer
to tap the
bricks into line

3 The third course is of soldier bricks, with the headers (ends) of the bricks facing forwards. In this course, alternate bricks should be centred on a joint underneath. Use the spirit level to check that the wall is vertical, and make any necessary corrections by gently tapping bricks into line using the handle of the mason's hammer. Build the fourth and fifth courses as for the first and second courses.

Third course
Lay the soldier
brick course,
with every
other brick
centred on the
vertical joints in
the course
underneath

Tile position
Arrange the tiles so that there is
an equal overhang at each side

Tile joints
Sandwich the tiles so that the joints are staggered

4 Lay the tiles on a 10 mm-thick bed of mortar, and avoid leaving any gaps in between them. Complete the first layer and proceed to the next. Start the second layer with half a tile (break with the mason's hammer) so that the joints between the rows of tiles are staggered.

Helpful hint

The shape and texture of the tiles will affect the appearance of the wall. Do not use concrete tiles (the edges are not decorative) or tiles that are very curved or smooth – both can be troublesome to work with.

Coping bricks
Bedded on their stretcher face

Pointing
Point the top joints so that they are smooth and flush

Frogs
Should all face in the same direction

Mortar
Angle the mortar down to the edge of the tiles

Protection
The idea of the coping bricks and tiles is that they make rain run off without touching the wall

5 Spread mortar along the top of the wall and lay the coping bricks on their stretcher face (side), with all the frogs facing in the same direction. Finish with the frog of the last brick facing inwards (so that the frog is not visible). Check that the coping is straight and level.

6 Clean up all the joints that still need doing and then concentrate on the mortar detail above the line of tiles. Spread mortar along the join and smooth it to form a sloped surface that is triangular in section (see drawing).

Storage seat

If your shed is bulging at the seams, this useful storage seat will provide a practical

and attractive solution. It also gives you the opportunity to build a decorative brick

box in the English diaper tradition (an all-over surface decoration of a small repeated

pattern such as diamonds or squares, using coloured, projecting or recessed bricks).

TIME

Three days if using an existing foundation.

SPECIAL TIPS

The seat is heavy. You may want to consider a hinged design.

YOU WILL NEED

Materials *for a storage seat 1.434 m long, 662 mm wide and 513 mm high*

• Bricks: 67 light-coloured bricks and 23 dark-coloured bricks
• Mortar: 1 part (10 kg) cement and 4 parts (40 kg) sand
• Wood: 2 pieces, 1.434 m long, 63 mm wide and 38 mm thick; and 6 pieces, 586 mm long, 63 mm wide and 38 mm thick (seat frame), 6 pieces, 1.434 m long, 100 mm wide and 20 mm thick (seat planks)

• Plywood (exterior grade): 1 piece, 1.434 m long, 662 mm wide and 5 mm thick (under-seat board)
• Nails: 16 x 100 mm (frame) and 36 x 50 mm (seat planks)

Tools
• Tape measure and a piece of chalk
• Shovel and mixing board, or cement mixer
• Wheelbarrow and bucket
• Bricklayer's trowel and pointing trowel
• Spirit level
• Mason's hammer
• General-purpose saw
• Claw hammer

ON THE BENCH

Have you ever looked at a plastic storage chest and thought that it would be really useful for the garden, but decided that it was far too ugly? Well, if you like good-looking, hard-working garden structures, this project might appeal to you. We have built the storage seat on the edge of a patio, where it can be used to hide away tools, pots and other paraphernalia, keeping them protected from the weather. The slatted seat is made from preserved pine, with an under-seat board of exterior plywood beneath the slats to stop rain getting into the storage space. Oak slats would look even better, but are more expensive. If you don't need storage space and just want a seat, you could make a lower structure and fashion the seat out of chunky railway sleepers. The diamond pattern of dark bricks is not difficult to achieve and can be altered if you want a different effect. Bands of different-coloured bricks, contrasting corner bricks, terracotta tiles and glazed tiles are some of the options open to you.

FRONT VIEW OF THE STORAGE SEAT

Light-coloured bricks

Build a foundation like this or use an existing foundation

Wooden seat
Protects contents from getting wet. Lifts off completely

Dark-coloured bricks
Use contrasting bricks for the pattern and the first course

Storage seat

EXPLODED VIEW OF THE STORAGE SEAT

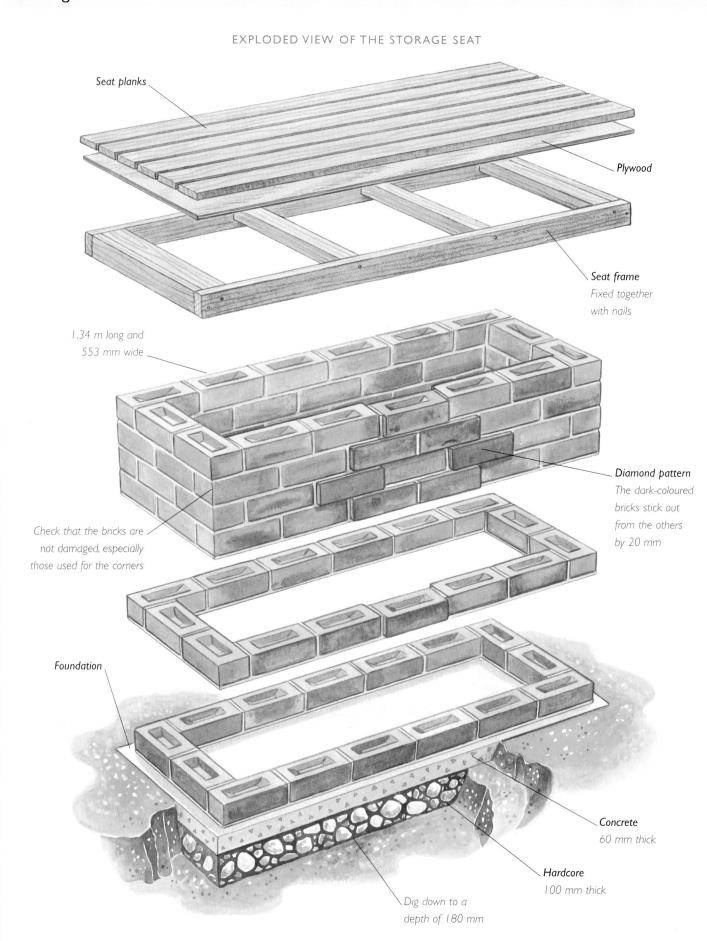

Seat planks

Plywood

Seat frame
*Fixed together
with nails*

*1.34 m long and
553 mm wide*

Diamond pattern
*The dark-coloured
bricks stick out
from the others
by 20 mm*

*Check that the bricks are
not damaged, especially
those used for the corners*

Foundation

Concrete
60 mm thick

Hardcore
100 mm thick

*Dig down to a
depth of 180 mm*

PLAN VIEW SHOWING THE FIRST COURSE OF BRICKS

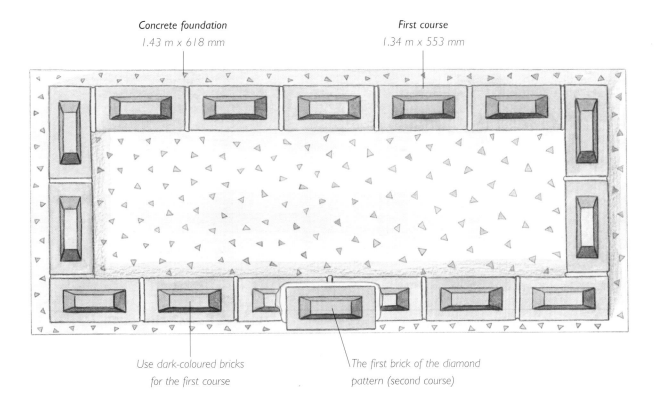

Concrete foundation
1.43 m x 618 mm

First course
1.34 m x 553 mm

Use dark-coloured bricks
for the first course

The first brick of the diamond
pattern (second course)

CUT-AWAY VIEW SHOWING THE WOOD SEAT

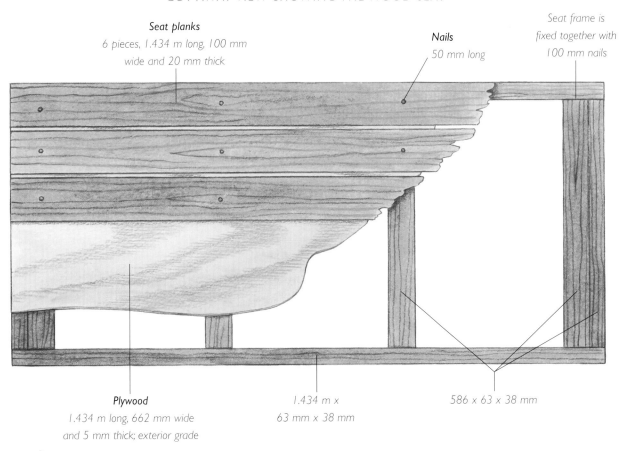

Seat planks
6 pieces, 1.434 m long, 100 mm
wide and 20 mm thick

Nails
50 mm long

Seat frame is
fixed together with
100 mm nails

Plywood
1.434 m long, 662 mm wide
and 5 mm thick; exterior grade

1.434 m x
63 mm x 38 mm

586 x 63 x 38 mm

Step-by-step: Making the storage seat

Spirit level
*Make sure that the
first course is level*

First course
*Bed the bricks
on a generous
layer of mortar*

1 Chalk out an area, 1.340 m long and 553 mm wide, on the foundation using the tape measure and a piece of wood for the seat frame. (See page 21 if using an existing foundation.) Lay the first course of dark bricks. Make sure that it is level, straight, and the joints are all 10 mm wide.

Helpful hint

If you change the size of the structure, try and keep to using whole bricks. If it is to be built against a wall, build it in the same way – don't be tempted to build just three sides, as it will make the structure very weak.

Second course
*Arrange the
second course
so that it is
staggered with
the first*

2 Continue laying the bricks, using the light-coloured bricks for the rest of the courses and the remaining dark bricks for the diamond pattern. The diamond bricks stick out from the others by 20 mm. Stagger the joints in each course.

Hammer
*Use the handle
to nudge and
adjust the bricks*

Mortar
Before removing excess mortar,
wait until it has partly dried

3 While building the courses, keep checking that the bricks are correctly positioned in a straight line, with equal gaps between them. Take extra care over the bricks used for the pattern, because any mistakes will be obvious. Use the spirit level to check the vertical alignment of the joints within the pattern.

Spirit level
Check the alignment of the bricks

Diaper bricks
The dark bricks forming the pattern need to project by 20 mm

Pointing
Slide slices of mortar into the joints

Seat planks
Nail them through the seat board and into the frame

Bricklayer's trowel
Use this as a work surface while you fill gaps with the pointing trowel

Seat board
Plywood sandwiched between the planks and the frame

Nails
Use two short nails at each end of the planks and one every so often along the length

4 Clean up all the joints, taking extra care on the front face of the structure and around the diamond pattern. Fill in any gaps, using the pointing trowel to slice slivers of mortar off a dollop of mortar held on the bricklayer's trowel, and force them into the cavity.

5 Build the seat to fit around the top of the wall (don't forget that the top brick of the diamond pattern sticks out by 20 mm). Assemble the seat frame using the long nails, lay the seat board on top of it, and cover it with equally spaced seat planks. Fix with the short nails.

Gateway columns

Get rid of decrepit, leaning wooden fence posts, or ugly concrete blocks, and build a noble gateway in the great country house tradition – a bold and dashing piece of garden architecture, which will make a splendid grand entrance to add class to your driveway or front path, or to any part of the garden. The distinctive ball finials magically transform straightforward columns into something special.

TIME
One day to prepare the foundation and three days to complete the columns.

SAFETY
If you build columns higher than these, you must also increase their width and depth.

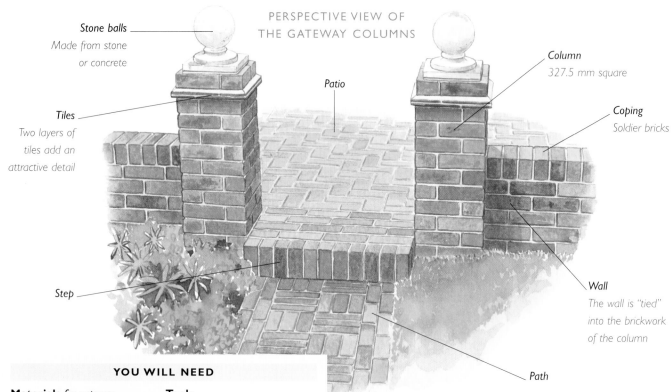

PERSPECTIVE VIEW OF
THE GATEWAY COLUMNS

Stone balls
Made from stone or concrete

Tiles
Two layers of tiles add an attractive detail

Step

Patio

Column
327.5 mm square

Coping
Soldier bricks

Wall
The wall is "tied" into the brickwork of the column

Path

YOU WILL NEED

Materials *for gateway columns 1.146 m high and 832 mm apart*
- Bricks: 172
- Tiles: 16 tiles, 220 mm long, 155 mm wide and 10 mm thick
- Stone or concrete balls: 2, 280 mm high, with a base 270 mm square
- Hardcore: 0.3 cu. metres
- Concrete: 1 part (120 kg) cement and 4 parts (480 kg) ballast
- Mortar: 1 part (20 kg) cement and 4 parts (80 kg) sand

Tools
- Tape measure, pegs, string, straight-edge and a piece of chalk
- Spade and fork
- Wheelbarrow and bucket
- Shovel and mixing board, or cement mixer
- Sledgehammer
- Bricklayer's trowel and pointing trowel
- Mason's hammer
- Bolster chisel
- Spirit level

MAKING A GRAND ENTRANCE

Stately homes often have ornate ironwork front gates hung from huge, formal pillars topped by a striking sculpture such as a giant stone eagle. These gateway columns are not quite so imposing, but they have the same classic pedigree and, in a more restrained way, look grand. We have built them to act as a visual divider between a patio and the rest of the garden, with the columns attached to low brick walls. The columns could also be used either side of a small gate in front of your house, or to span a flight of steps in a terraced garden. They can be used as a feature anywhere in the garden – for example wherever there is a pathway leading from one distinct area of the garden to another, or where there is a change in levels, you can build columns and divide off the area by adding a brick wall, wooden picket fence or a beautiful hedge.

Gateway columns

EXPLODED VIEW OF THE GATEWAY COLUMNS

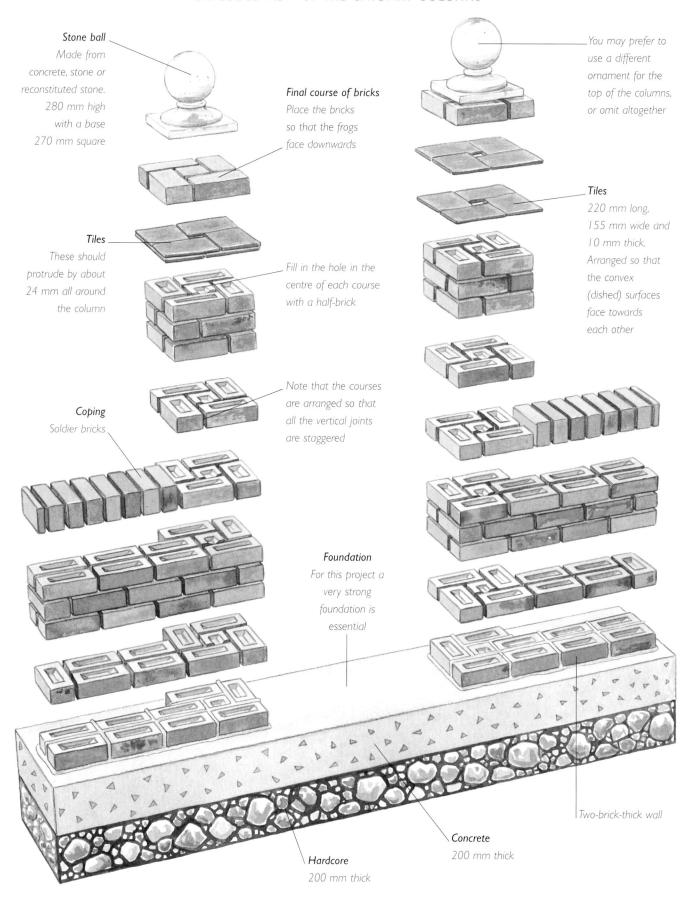

Stone ball
Made from concrete, stone or reconstituted stone. 280 mm high with a base 270 mm square

Final course of bricks
Place the bricks so that the frogs face downwards

You may prefer to use a different ornament for the top of the columns, or omit altogether

Tiles
220 mm long, 155 mm wide and 10 mm thick. Arranged so that the convex (dished) surfaces face towards each other

Tiles
These should protrude by about 24 mm all around the column

Fill in the hole in the centre of each course with a half-brick

Note that the courses are arranged so that all the vertical joints are staggered

Coping
Soldier bricks

Foundation
For this project a very strong foundation is essential

Two-brick-thick wall

Concrete
200 mm thick

Hardcore
200 mm thick

FRONT VIEW OF THE GATEWAY COLUMNS

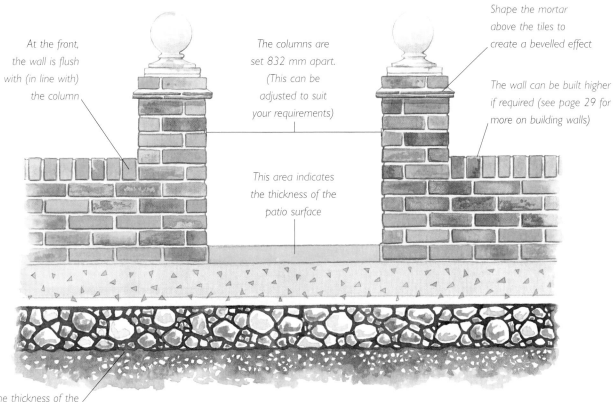

At the front, the wall is flush with (in line with) the column

The columns are set 832 mm apart. (This can be adjusted to suit your requirements)

Shape the mortar above the tiles to create a bevelled effect

The wall can be built higher if required (see page 29 for more on building walls)

This area indicates the thickness of the patio surface

The thickness of the foundation can be reduced if the ground in your garden is unusually hard

BACK VIEW OF THE GATEWAY COLUMNS

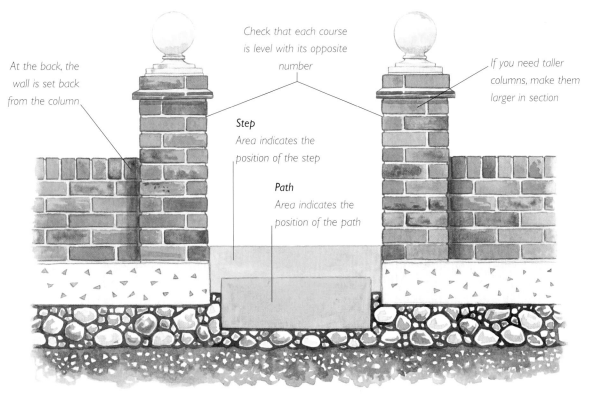

At the back, the wall is set back from the column

Check that each course is level with its opposite number

If you need taller columns, make them larger in section

Step
Area indicates the position of the step

Path
Area indicates the position of the path

Step-by-step: **Making the gateway columns**

Bonds
*Study the working
drawing carefully*

Spirit level
*Check that
each brick is
correctly
positioned
before placing
the next one.
Ensure that
the corners of
the column
are true*

1 Plan the columns and adjoining walls. If you need steps between the columns, see page 30. Build a foundation using at least 200 mm of concrete over 200 mm of compacted hardcore. Mark out the first course and practise laying the bricks without mortar. Lay two courses with mortar, making checks as you go.

Helpful hint

An inadequate foundation (too narrow, too thin or badly made) may cause a pillar to crack or lean. If in doubt, build a bigger foundation than you think is needed.

Pointing
*Point the joints
to a raked finish*

Mortar
*Ideally, excess
mortar should
be left alone
until it is has
dried to a
crumbly texture*

Soldier brick coping
*Lay the bricks on their
stretcher face*

*Pointing the
wall face*
*Fill any gaps.
Rake out the
mortar to
create a
weathered
finish*

*Pointing the
soldier bricks*
*Point the
coping to a
smooth finish*

2 During construction of the columns, clean up the joints between the bricks using the tip of the pointing trowel. Try not to smear mortar on the surface of the bricks (especially wet mortar), and avoid raking out too much mortar from between the bricks.

3 Complete laying the courses of the low brick walls, and continue building the columns for another two courses. Lay a coping of soldier bricks, starting at the column end. Use the spirit level and handle of the mason's hammer to push the coping into alignment. Clean up the wall joints.

Tiles
Old roof tiles are perfect for this

Arrangment
Sandwich the tiles in place so that the joints are staggered

Tile overhang
Make sure that the overhang is equal all the way round

4 Continue building the columns, all the time checking that the courses in each column are level with each other and the sides and corners of the columns are vertical. Bed two layers of tiles on mortar in the pattern shown. Note that if the tiles are curved, they should be placed so that the first layer curves upwards and the second layer curves downwards (and the joints need to be staggered).

Ball finial
Dampen the base of the finial prior to bedding it on mortar

Frogs
The bricks at the top of the column are placed with the frog facing downwards

5 Build a final course of bricks on top of the tiles, but this time turn the bricks so the frogs are facing downwards. Practise positioning the balls on top of the columns, and when you have established the correct position, draw around them with chalk. Spread a layer of mortar inside the marked area and lower the balls into place. Inspect all the brickwork for any gaps that need filling, and clean up the joints as necessary.

Strawberry barrel

How many times have you planted out your strawberries, only to find them eradicated by a slithering army of slugs? This strawberry barrel will help provide a defence by literally lifting your strawberries up to a new level, making access harder for predators. The strawberries are also easier to pick from their elevated position, and make an attractive feature draped over the brickwork.

TIME

One day for the foundation and four days to complete the barrel.

SPECIAL TIPS

Don't be tempted to build without a trammel, because the results will be disappointing.

YOU WILL NEED

Materials *for a strawberry barrel 1.153 m high and 752 mm in diameter*
- Bricks: 117
- Slate: 12 pieces, 225 mm long, 166 mm wide and 6 mm thick
- Pebbles: 400, 15–20 mm in diameter
- Hardcore: 0.1 cu. metres
- Concrete: 1 part (30 kg) cement and 4 parts (120 kg) ballast
- Mortar: 1 part (25 kg) cement and 4 parts (100 kg) sand
- Wood: 1 piece, 412 mm long, 65 mm wide and 25 mm thick (trammel)
- Metal tube: 1.666 m long and 27 mm in diameter (trammel)
- Land drainage pipe: 1 m long, 100 mm in diameter (to help water drainage in the soil)

Tools
- Tape measure, pegs and string
- Spade
- Wheelbarrow and bucket
- Shovel and mixing board, or cement mixer
- Sledgehammer
- Mason's hammer and club hammer

- Spirit level
- Drill and bit to match diameter of the metal tube
- Mole grips
- Bolster chisel
- Bricklayer's trowel and pointing trowel
- Rubber mallet
- Tile cutter

A STRAWBERRY PASSION

This sculptural planter is specifically designed for growing strawberries and presenting them in a decorative way. It is probably best to build it in a sunny spot to one side of the garden, or as the centrepiece of a vegetable patch or decorative cottage garden. If you intend to use the structure to plant flowers instead, you may want to incorporate more pockets, and reserve the shady side for plants that don't need as much sun.

The height of the barrel can be reduced if required. The whole barrel is built using half-bricks, so choose bricks that break in half easily. The structure looks complicated, but it is in fact simple to build as the trammel (see page 27) seems to do all the work for you. Make the strawberry barrel something to be proud of – take care over the joints and don't skimp on the decorative pebbles pressed into the mortar.

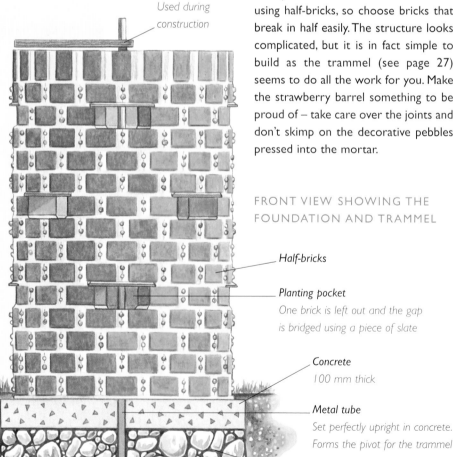

Trammel
Used during construction

FRONT VIEW SHOWING THE FOUNDATION AND TRAMMEL

Half-bricks

Planting pocket
One brick is left out and the gap is bridged using a piece of slate

Concrete
100 mm thick

Metal tube
Set perfectly upright in concrete. Forms the pivot for the trammel

Hardcore
150 mm thick

Strawberry barrel

EXPLODED VIEW OF THE STRAWBERRY BARREL

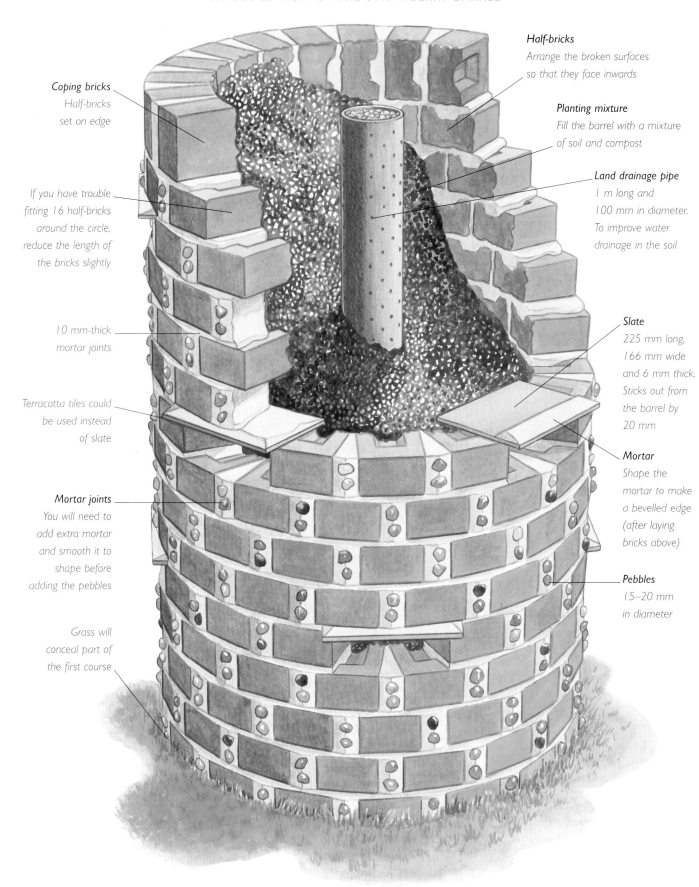

Half-bricks
Arrange the broken surfaces
so that they face inwards

Coping bricks
Half-bricks
set on edge

Planting mixture
Fill the barrel with a mixture
of soil and compost

Land drainage pipe
1 m long and
100 mm in diameter.
To improve water
drainage in the soil

If you have trouble
fitting 16 half-bricks
around the circle,
reduce the length of
the bricks slightly

Slate
225 mm long,
166 mm wide
and 6 mm thick.
Sticks out from
the barrel by
20 mm

10 mm-thick
mortar joints

Terracotta tiles could
be used instead
of slate

Mortar
Shape the
mortar to make
a bevelled edge
(after laying
bricks above)

Mortar joints
You will need to
add extra mortar
and smooth it to
shape before
adding the pebbles

Pebbles
15–20 mm
in diameter

Grass will
conceal part of
the first course

PLAN VIEW SHOWING THE TRAMMEL AND A COMPLETE COURSE OF BRICKS

Concrete
845 mm square,
100 mm thick.
Set on 150 mm
of hardcore

Metal tube
Set perfectly
upright in the
concrete.
Check it is
vertical by using
a spirit level

376 mm

Trammel arm
412 mm long,
65 mm wide
and 25 mm thick.
Use the trammel
to help you
position the
bricks accurately

Mortar
The wide gaps
between the bricks
need to be carefully
filled with mortar

PLAN VIEW SHOWING THE LAYOUT OF THE SLATES OVER THE PLANTING POCKETS

After each course
of bricks, raise the
trammel by 75 mm
(the thickness of a
brick plus 10 mm
of mortar) and
support it at the
centre by clamping
a pair of mole grips
underneath it

Position the slate
so that it sticks out
from the side of
the barrel by
20 mm. Use the
trammel as a guide

The slate should
be placed centrally
over the pocket of
space beneath

Step-by-step: **Making the strawberry barrel**

Mole grips
Slide up the tube until the trammel
arm is at the correct height

Positioning
Set each brick square with
the end of the trammel

Trammel arm
Establishes the
correct position
for the bricks

Drainage
The wood
ensures an
open joint
for drainage

Levelling
Tap the
trammel
until the brick
is level

1 Build a level foundation. While the concrete is still wet, knock the metal tube into the centre of the foundation. Check that it is vertical using the spirit level. When the concrete is dry, make a trammel (see page 27). This trammel pivots on the metal tube. Use mole grips to hold the trammel arm up. Practise laying the first course of half-bricks and check that you can fit sixteen around the circle.

2 Mix up the mortar and start laying the first course of bricks, bedding them level on 10 mm-thick mortar and using the trammel as a positional guide. Leave a scrap of wood between two of the bricks to create a water drainage hole (pull out on completion). Use the rubber mallet, on top of the end of the trammel arm, to knock the bricks down. Check that the course is level with the spirit level.

3 Continue building further courses. After each course is complete, create angled mortar joints between the bricks and push two small pebbles into each one. This takes a bit of practice to get right, so be prepared to scrape out the first few joints and start over again.

Mortar
Angle a wedge
of mortar
between the
bricks

Decoration
Push the
pebbles into
the soft mortar

Mole grips
Slide the grips up until
level with the slate

Slate
Push the
slate outwards
so that it
overhangs by
about 20 mm

4 Continue building upwards until you get to the fifth course. On this course, leave out four bricks to create each planting pocket. Cut pieces of slate or imitation slate and use these to bridge the gaps, the slate sticking out from the barrel by 20 mm. After laying the next course, spread mortar over the part of the slate that sticks out.

Helpful hint

Take care when fitting the pieces of slate – position them so that sharp edges face inwards, or smooth the edges and corners with an angle grinder. Clay tiles could be used instead of slate.

Soldier course
Arrange the
half-bricks on
their stretcher
face for a
decorative
finish

5 After each course that includes planting pockets, lay three complete courses of bricks before the next course of planting pockets. After completing three courses with planting pockets, creating a total of twelve pockets, build a final course of bricks on top, followed by a soldier course. Fill all the joints with mortar, finish them with the pointing trowel, and stud with pebbles (not on the soldier course). After a few days, remove the metal tube by repeatedly bending it until it snaps off. Put a layer of crocks in the bottom of the barrel for drainage, followed by the drainage pipe. Hold it upright as you fill the strawberry barrel with soil. Plant the pockets with strawberry plants.

Semicircular steps

You might think that a doorstep is just a block of brickwork that enables you to move easily from one level to another, but that is only part of its function. Front doorsteps are traditionally built to make a grand, welcoming feature. The curved form of these steps makes attractive terracing, where there is plenty of space to set out a display of pot plants to make the entrance to the house look even more appealing.

TIME

Four days to build (five if you need a foundation).

SAFETY

Ensure that the surface of the steps is smooth, with no slightly raised areas that might cause people to trip. The steps must be correctly spaced for your site. (See page 30.)

YOU WILL NEED

Materials *for semicircular steps 2.165 m long, 1.04 m wide and 298 mm high*
- Bricks: 168
- Hardcore: 0.25 cu. metres
- Concrete: 1 part (100 kg) cement; 4 parts (400 kg) ballast
- Mortar: 1 part (20 kg) cement and 4 parts (80 kg) sand
- Wood: 1 piece, 3 m long, 35 mm wide and 20 mm thick (straight-edge and trammel); 1 piece, 300 mm long and 75 mm square, and 1 piece, 450 mm long, 100 mm wide and 50 mm thick (tamping beams)
- Masonry nails: 2 x 145 mm (trammel pivot and guide)

Tools
- Tape measure and chalk
- Spade
- Wheelbarrow and bucket
- Shovel and mixing board, or cement mixer
- Sledgehammer
- Claw hammer
- Spirit level
- Bricklayer's trowel and pointing trowel
- Mason's hammer, bolster chisel

A STEP UP FROM THE REST

First impressions count – or at least that is what people say when they meet somebody new – and the same applies to the entrance to your house. These decorative steps, with an interesting patterned surface, will definitely make a good impression, and their generous size provides a comfortable standing area.

When planning steps, one of the most important factors is the height of each step (the riser measurement). Steps should be no greater than 230 mm high, and no less than 60 mm high (a good average would be 150 mm).

You may need to adjust the design to suit your site (see page 30 about planning steps). If you have a paved surface surrounding the area of the steps, consider how you will repair it after the job is finished.

Mark out and build a concrete foundation that slopes away from the house slightly (about 25 mm per 2 m): remove existing paving and dig a foundation 200 mm deep, fill it with compacted hardcore 100 mm thick, and top with 100 mm of concrete.

CROSS-SECTION DETAIL OF THE SEMICIRCULAR STEPS

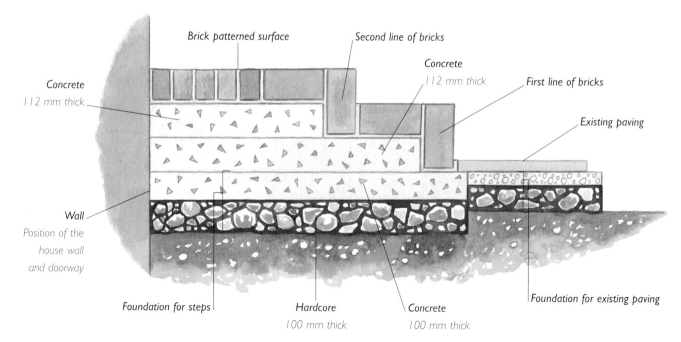

Brick patterned surface

Second line of bricks

Concrete
112 mm thick

First line of bricks

Concrete
112 mm thick

Existing paving

Wall

Position of the house wall and doorway

Foundation for steps

Hardcore
100 mm thick

Concrete
100 mm thick

Foundation for existing paving

Semicircular steps

PLAN VIEW OF THE SEMICIRCULAR STEPS

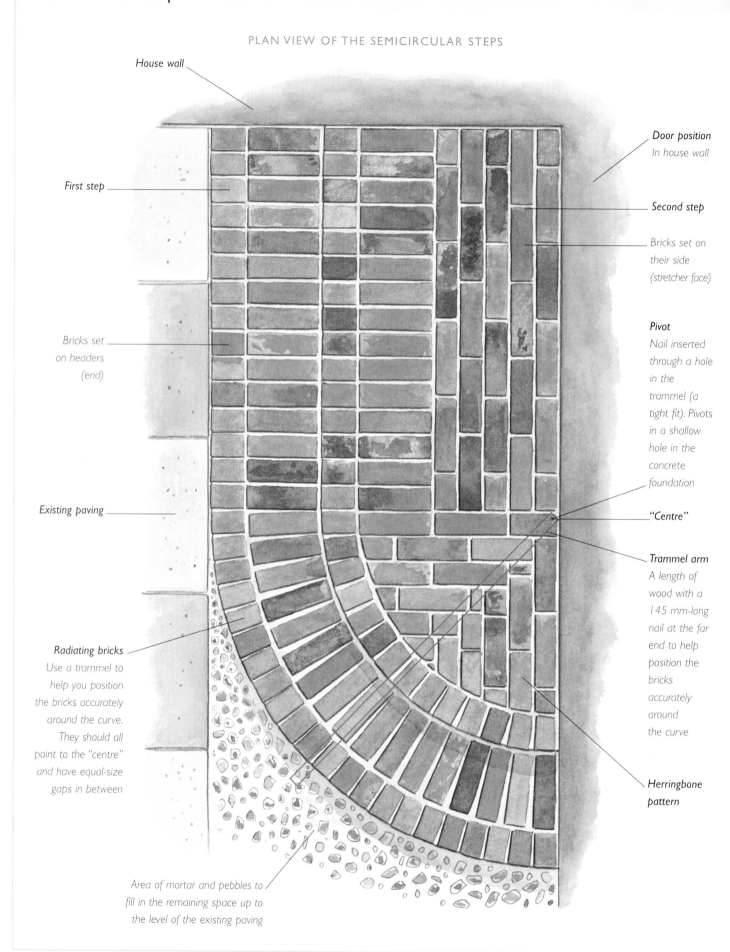

House wall

Door position
In house wall

First step

Second step

Bricks set on their side (stretcher face)

Bricks set
on headers
(end)

Pivot
Nail inserted
through a hole
in the
trammel (a
tight fit). Pivots
in a shallow
hole in the
concrete
foundation

Existing paving

"Centre"

Trammel arm
*A length of
wood with a
145 mm-long
nail at the far
end to help
position the
bricks
accurately
around
the curve*

Radiating bricks
*Use a trammel to
help you position
the bricks accurately
around the curve.
They should all
point to the "centre"
and have equal-size
gaps in between*

Herringbone
pattern

*Area of mortar and pebbles to
fill in the remaining space up to
the level of the existing paving*

EXPLODED VIEW OF THE SEMICIRCULAR STEPS

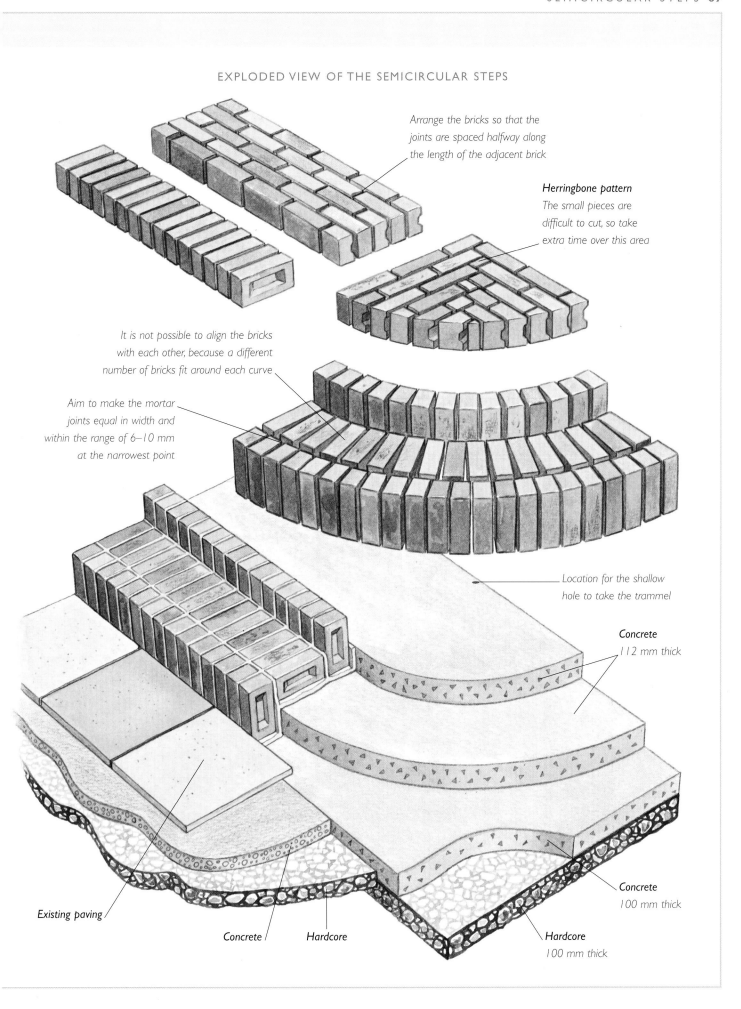

Arrange the bricks so that the joints are spaced halfway along the length of the adjacent brick

Herringbone pattern
The small pieces are difficult to cut, so take extra time over this area

It is not possible to align the bricks with each other, because a different number of bricks fit around each curve

Aim to make the mortar joints equal in width and within the range of 6–10 mm at the narrowest point

Location for the shallow hole to take the trammel

Concrete
112 mm thick

Existing paving

Concrete

Hardcore

Concrete
100 mm thick

Hardcore
100 mm thick

Step-by-step: **Making the semicircular steps**

Soldier bricks
Set the bricks upright on their header face

Concrete
Depth must allow for (on top) a brick on its side plus 10 mm

Trammel
Has a hanging nail to facilitate the aligning of the bricks

Tamping
Use waste wood to tamp the concrete level

Outer edge of bottom step
Area within is filled with concrete

1 Build the outer edge of the bottom step from soldier bricks set on end, using the trammel (see page 27) and spirit level to guide you. Butter the frog face with mortar, and lay each brick on 10 mm of mortar. The straight bricks have 10 mm of mortar between them, and the bricks following the curve have a minimum of 10 mm of mortar between them.

2 Fill the area within the outer edge with concrete to a level depth that leaves room for a layer of bricks on their stretcher face plus 10 mm of mortar. Use the shorter tamping beam to spread the concrete and check that it is level. If in doubt, it is better to err on the side of having the concrete a bit lower (and later use extra mortar to build up the bricks to the correct level). Leave the concrete to dry.

Alignment
The bricks must point towards the "centre" of the trammel

Trammel
Check the alignment of every brick

Step level
Ensure that the soldier bricks are upright

3 Spread a bed of mortar over the concrete and use the trammel and spirit level to help you lay the curve of bricks. The gaps between the bricks won't line up with the outer edge, but try to maintain equal-thickness gaps, and make sure all the bricks around the curve point to the "centre" (see working drawing).

4 Build the outer edge of the top step on the same slab of concrete and again use the trammel to guide you around the curve. Check that the tops of the bricks are level with the bottom of the doorway. Allow the mortar between the bricks to dry before proceeding to the next stage.

Concrete
Depth must allow for (on top) a
brick on its side plus 10 mm

Tamping
Tamp the
concrete level

Brick level
Keep checking
that the bricks
remain true

 Fill the area inside the outer edge of the top step with concrete as described in step 2. Tamp with the longer tamping beam. There should be enough space to lay the final bricks on a 10 mm-thick bed of mortar.

Pattern
This area of
pattern is what
people will notice
first when they
approach your
door. If you are
worried about
fitting the bricks
into the space, or
think you might
make a mistake,
practise setting
out the bricks in
the design before
spreading mortar

6 When the concrete has set, fill in the top step with bricks in the two patterns illustrated. Lay the straight line of staggered bricks first, then finish with the 90° pattern that fills the curved area. Cut the bricks to shape using the mason's hammer and bolster chisel. Fill the joints with a dryish mixture of mortar and tidy them up with the pointing trowel.

Helpful hint

When you are levelling the bricks, try to make them end up sloping away from the house slightly.

Inspirations: Brick steps

Nothing beats bricks for versatility when it comes to building steps. They can be set with the frog face or the bottom face uppermost, on their end (header) or on their side (stretcher) in order to create different effects and levels. They can be cut or angled, and laid in a variety of patterns on the treads. Bricks harmonize with stone and tiles – designs for steps can successfully comprise a mixture of materials. Best of all, bricks are wonderfully easy to handle and make step-building a pleasure.

FAR RIGHT This solidly well-built flight of steps connects a path to a beautiful brick courtyard. The design appears effortless, but in fact great care has gone into planning the overall brickwork scheme and incorporating steps that are subtly curved.

ABOVE A decorative, low-rise set of two steps in a country garden. Notice how the shape and sweeping arrangement of the steps leads the eye across the patio to the other steps and the lawn beyond. The framed herringbone pattern and recessed detailing must have been a challenge to build.

RIGHT This step started life as a small step (the two-brick-wide section near the door). When the owner wanted the step made deeper, the bricklayer simply added a band of clay roof tiles set on edge plus another row of bricks on edge. The tiles add decorative interest to what would otherwise be a plain step.

Tudor arch wall niche

A niche in a wall always invites questions. What is it for? Is it a shrine? Is it a blocked-up window? When was it built? So if you want to create a bit of intrigue in your garden, this project is ideal. In Tudor times, bricks first came to be used in a decorative way, and this niche has been inspired by Tudor arches. It is an exciting but complex project to build – an enjoyably skill-testing challenge.

TIME

Six days (do not lay more than four courses in one day).

SAFETY

See page 29 for information on walls and requirements for piers and buttresses.

YOU WILL NEED

Materials *for Tudor arch wall niche 1.61 m high and 1.453 m wide*
- Bricks: 276
- Stone slab: 1 piece, 554 mm long, 250 mm wide and 40 mm thick (sill)
- Hardcore: 0.1 cu. metres
- Sand: 1 shovelful
- Concrete: 1 part (30 kg) cement and 4 parts (120 kg) ballast
- Mortar: 1 part (30 kg) cement and 4 parts (120 kg) sand
- Wood: 10 pieces, 85 mm long, 30 mm wide and 22 mm thick (sticks for centre of former); 1 piece, 700 mm long, 35 mm wide and 22 mm thick (trammel)
- Plywood: 2 pieces, 563 mm long, 122 mm wide and 6 mm thick (former)
- Nails: 20 x 40 mm

Tools
- Tape measure, pegs, string, straight-edge and piece of chalk
- Spade
- Wheelbarrow and bucket
- Shovel and mixing board, or cement mixer
- Sledgehammer
- Bricklayer's trowel and pointing trowel
- Mason's hammer and club hammer
- Bolster chisel
- Rubber mallet
- Spirit level
- General-purpose saw
- Jigsaw
- Claw hammer

A FINE DISPLAY

The recess or niche is decorative in itself, but it also acts like a picture frame for anything you want to display in it. We have put a statuette in this one, but yours could display a mosaic picture, salvaged cartwheel or curious antique. Other ideas include a wall mask fixed in the recess, spouting water into a stone trough, or the whole arch can be built deeper and bigger and the sill made into a narrow seat for perching on – a kind of brick arbour.

This project is a little more challenging than the others, because you need to keep all the vertical joints in the coursework aligned. This ensures that the sides of the archway are well presented. However, the finished results are well worth the effort.

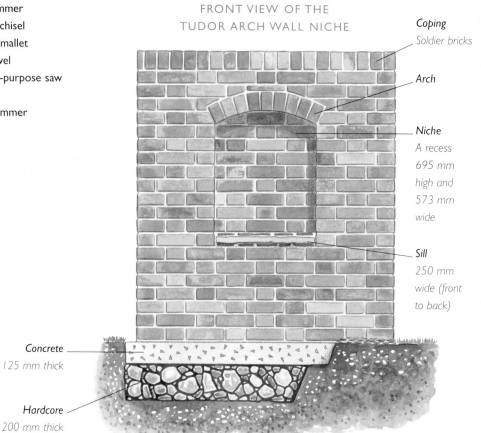

FRONT VIEW OF THE TUDOR ARCH WALL NICHE

Coping
Soldier bricks

Arch

Niche
A recess 695 mm high and 573 mm wide

Sill
250 mm wide (front to back)

Concrete
125 mm thick

Hardcore
200 mm thick

Tudor arch wall niche

FRONT VIEW OF THE ARCH FORMER (ONE SIDE REMOVED)

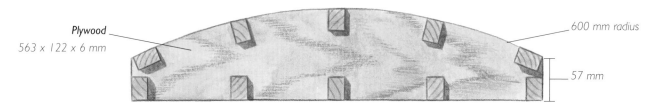

Plywood
563 x 122 x 6 mm

600 mm radius

57 mm

EXPLODED VIEW OF THE ARCH FORMER

Sticks
85 x 30 x 22 mm

Sticks
Arrange the sticks around the shape at roughly the intervals shown (fix with nails)

Nail the second side to the ends of the sticks, making sure that the shapes are aligned with each other

FRONT VIEW SHOWING HOW TO SUPPORT THE FORMER

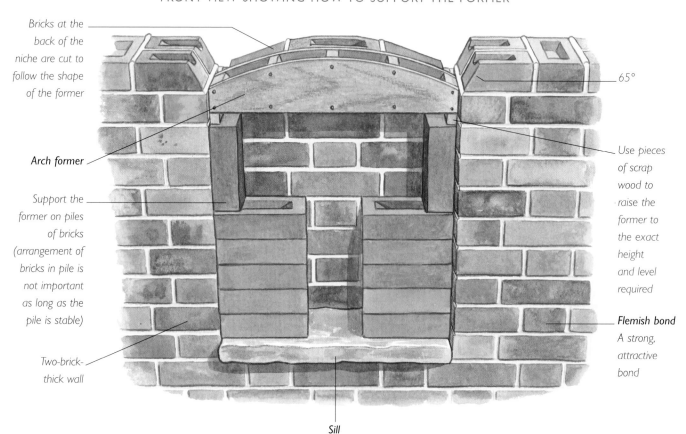

Bricks at the back of the niche are cut to follow the shape of the former

Arch former

Support the former on piles of bricks (arrangement of bricks in pile is not important as long as the pile is stable)

Two-brick-thick wall

65°

Use pieces of scrap wood to raise the former to the exact height and level required

Flemish bond
A strong, attractive bond

Sill
Stone slab, 554 x 250 x 40 mm

EXPLODED VIEW OF THE TUDOR ARCH WALL NICHE

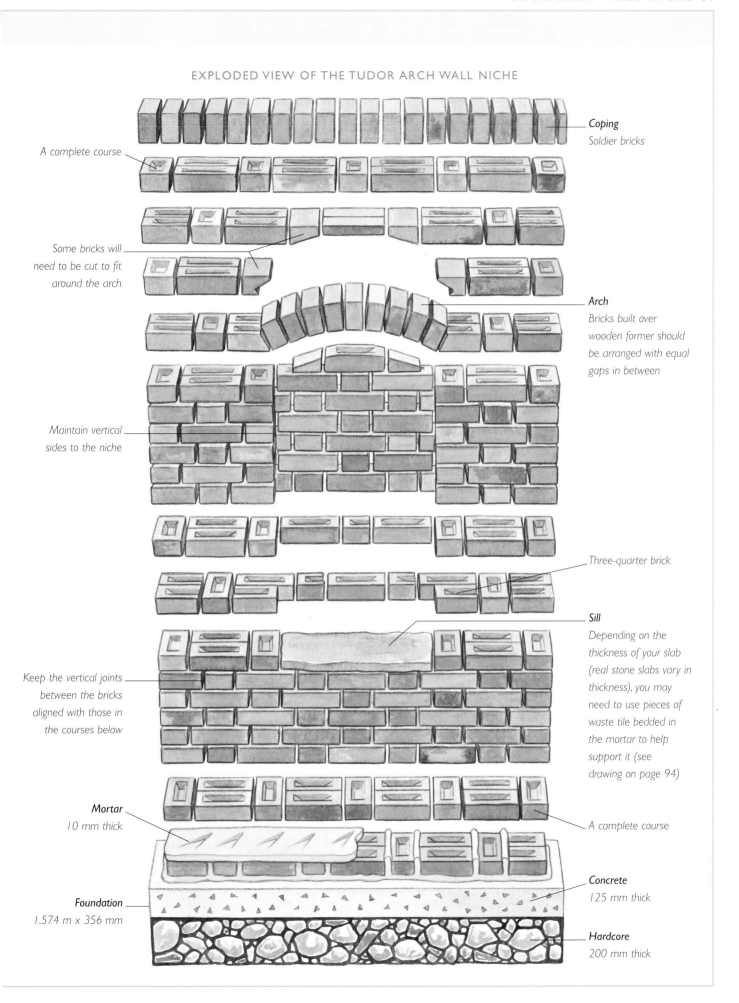

Coping
Soldier bricks

A complete course

*Some bricks will
need to be cut to fit
around the arch*

Arch
Bricks built over
wooden former should
be arranged with equal
gaps in between

*Maintain vertical
sides to the niche*

Three-quarter brick

Sill
Depending on the
thickness of your slab
(real stone slabs vary in
thickness), you may
need to use pieces of
waste tile bedded in
the mortar to help
support it (see
drawing on page 94)

*Keep the vertical joints
between the bricks
aligned with those in
the courses below*

Mortar
10 mm thick

A complete course

Concrete
125 mm thick

Foundation
1.574 m x 356 mm

Hardcore
200 mm thick

Step-by-step: Making the Tudor arch wall niche

Wall
*Build a base wall to
the required sill height*

Bond
*Flemish bond
results in an
extremely
strong bond*

I Build a foundation 1.574 mm long and 356 mm wide, consisting of a 200 mm-thick layer of hardcore topped with a 125 mm-thick layer of concrete. When the concrete is dry, lay the first course of bricks. Note that this wall is two bricks thick, and is built using Flemish bond. Continue building the wall until you have completed seven courses. Use a straight-edge, spirit level and rubber mallet to help double-check the level and straightness of the wall. Scrape out and clean the joints before the mortar dries.

Levelling
*Use mortar, and
if necessary
scraps of slate,
to ensure the
sill is level*

2 On the eighth course, leave a central space for the slab. Check that your stone sill is the correct size by placing it on the wall. The ends should align with joints between the bricks of the sixth course (if not, cut to size). Position the slab on a generous bed of mortar and coat it with sand to protect the surface during the rest of the building operation. The slab protrudes from the wall by 36 mm.

Sill
*Ease the sill
outwards so
that it protrudes
by 36 mm*

Single-thickness wall
Use half-bricks to create the
illusion of a Flemish bond

Former
The former can be rough and
ready, as long as it does the job

Corners
Make sure that
the corners are
vertically true

Alignment
The curved
pieces must be
aligned with
each other

Plywood
Draw the shape
of the former by
using a grid to
plot the curve, or
use a trammel
to draw an arc
with a radius of
600 mm

3 Continue building upwards for a
further eight courses, reducing the
wall to a single thickness at the back of the
slab, creating a niche. Study the working
drawings to see how the bricks are placed
for the best effect.

4 Build a wooden former to support
the arch during construction. (See
page 27 for information about trammels.)
Cut out the pieces with the jigsaw and join
together – place one of the sticks
underneath and hammer through the
plywood into the stick. Nail on the rest of
the sticks in the same way, then put the
other sheet of plywood on top, and nail
through into the sticks.

Practice
It is a good idea to
practise arranging
bricks on top of
the former. Once
you have a feel for
the gaps it is
necessary to leave
between each
brick, it is more
likely that you will
arrange them
correctly when
building with
mortar. Angle them
so they are all
aimed at a central
point on the sill.

5 Support the former on piles
of bricks. Continue building
the single-brick-thick wall behind
it, cutting bricks to follow the
shape of the curve. Complete the
course either side of the arch
using angled bricks to support it
(see diagram). Lay the top of the
arch over the former, maintaining
equal gaps between the bricks.
Build two courses above the
arch, cutting bricks as necessary.
Finish with a soldier brick coping.

Helpful hint

You risk damaging the
formwork if you knock the
bricks too hard. It is better
to take your time applying
the correct amount of
mortar to each brick.

Classic round pond

There is something complete and rather satisfying about a circular pool of water.

This sunken pond is interesting to build and makes a beautiful feature that will suit

most styles of garden. We have built it to fit snugly into a patio, where it can be

surrounded by an ever-changing display of container plants to give the pond a

distinct seasonal character.

TIME

Two days to dig the hole and four to five days to complete the brickwork.

SPECIAL TIPS

If you have young children, it is better not to have a pond in your garden.

YOU WILL NEED

Materials *for a pond 2.016 m in diameter and 900 mm deep*
- Bricks: 220 (walls) and 47 (top edge)
- Concrete: 1 part (72 kg) cement and 4 parts (288 kg) ballast
- Mortar: 1 part (50 kg) cement and 3 parts (150 kg) sand
- Soft sand: 1 tonne
- Wood:
  1 piece, 1.9 m long, 90 mm wide and 60 mm thick, and 2 pieces, 1.2 m long, 90 mm wide and 30 mm thick (tamping beam with handles);
  1 piece, 200 mm long, 75 mm wide and 75 mm thick (trammel support block);
  1 piece, 1.295 m long, 65 mm wide and 30 mm thick (trammel arm);
  and 1 piece, 1.84 m long, 90 mm wide and 30 mm thick (beam to check level)
- Plywood: 1 piece, 500 mm square and 6 mm thick (trammel base), and 1 piece, 467 mm long, 305 mm wide and 6 mm thick (U-shaped trammel piece)
- Geo-textile: 37 sq. metres
- Butyl liner: 1 piece, 4.3 m square
- Nails: 5 x 60 mm

Tools
- Tape measure, pegs, string, marking chalk or spray marker
- Spade and fork
- Wheelbarrow and bucket
- Scissors
- General-purpose saw
- Claw hammer
- Shovel and mixing board, or cement mixer
- Jigsaw
- Portable workbench
- Bricklayer's trowel and pointing trowel
- Mason's hammer
- Spirit level
- Sledgehammer

LAYOUT OF THE FIRST COURSE OF BRICKS

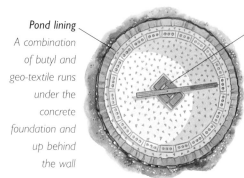

Pond lining
A combination of butyl and geo-textile runs under the concrete foundation and up behind the wall

Trammel
Use a length of wood pivoted at the centre of the pond to indicate the correct positioning of the wall bricks (see also page 27)

LAYOUT OF THE TOP EDGE BRICKS

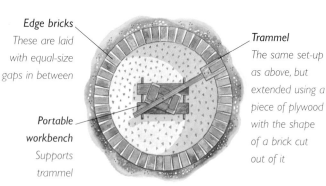

Edge bricks
These are laid with equal-size gaps in between

Portable workbench
Supports trammel

Trammel
The same set-up as above, but extended using a piece of plywood with the shape of a brick cut out of it

CIRCLE POWER

This round, sunken brick pond is a classic. A pond often becomes the focal point of a garden or courtyard, and can be treated in different ways – you can populate it with fish, plant a glorious display of water-lilies, or install a water feature.

There are important safety factors to take into account if you are considering building a pond. If you have young children, it is safer not to have a pond. (To protect visiting children, make a slatted wooden lid to cover the pond for short periods.)

Avoid excavating areas where there is a likelihood of uncovering pipes and drains – as a general rule, always dig carefully and if you encounter any, seek expert advice. (See also page 38.) If you want to install a fountain, incorporate armoured plastic pipe (50 mm in diameter) to protect the pump cable, which will run across the bottom of the pond (on top of the liner), through a hole in the wall, up between the wall and the liner, over the edge of the liner, and then be buried under paving slabs.

Classic round pond

CUT-AWAY CROSS-SECTION VIEW OF THE CLASSIC ROUND POND

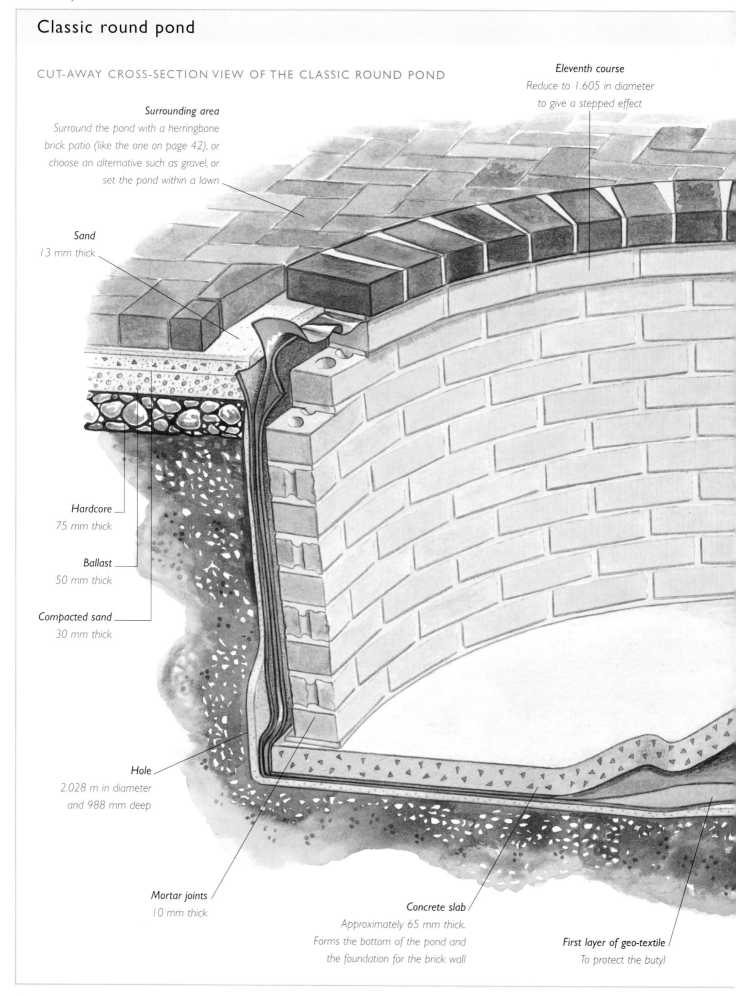

Eleventh course
Reduce to 1.605 in diameter to give a stepped effect

Surrounding area
Surround the pond with a herringbone brick patio (like the one on page 42), or choose an alternative such as gravel, or set the pond within a lawn

Sand
13 mm thick

Hardcore
75 mm thick

Ballast
50 mm thick

Compacted sand
30 mm thick

Hole
2.028 m in diameter and 988 mm deep

Mortar joints
10 mm thick

Concrete slab
Approximately 65 mm thick. Forms the bottom of the pond and the foundation for the brick wall

First layer of geo-textile
To protect the butyl

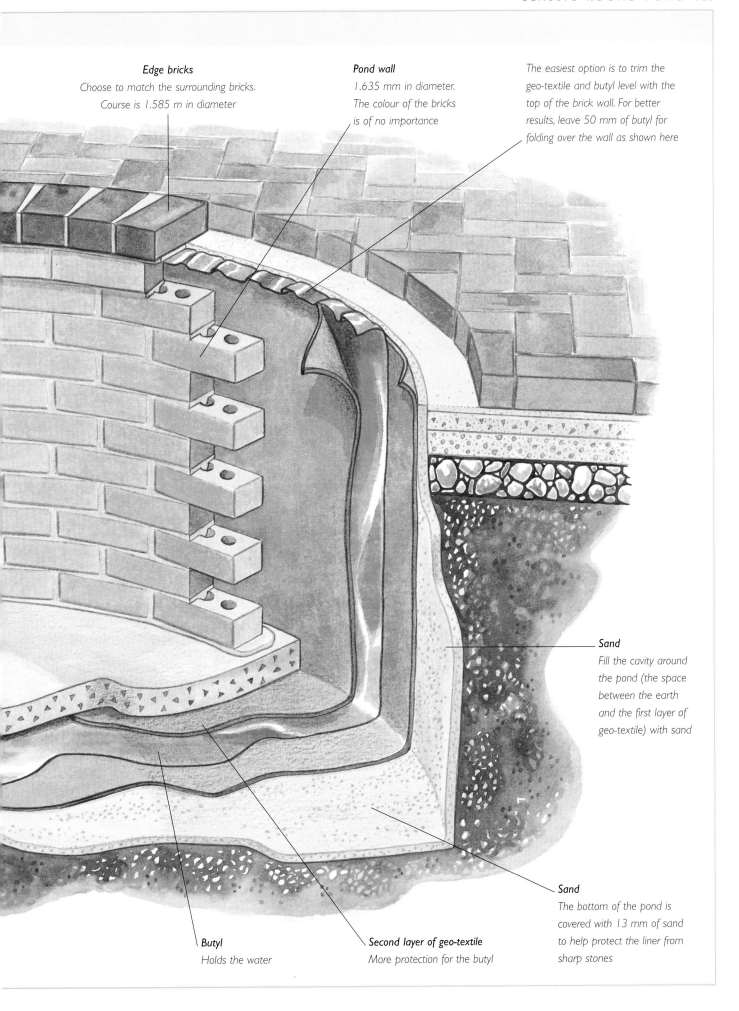

Edge bricks
Choose to match the surrounding bricks.
Course is 1.585 m in diameter

Pond wall
1.635 mm in diameter.
The colour of the bricks
is of no importance

The easiest option is to trim the
geo-textile and butyl level with the
top of the brick wall. For better
results, leave 50 mm of butyl for
folding over the wall as shown here

Sand
Fill the cavity around
the pond (the space
between the earth
and the first layer of
geo-textile) with sand

Sand
The bottom of the pond is
covered with 13 mm of sand
to help protect the liner from
sharp stones

Butyl
Holds the water

Second layer of geo-textile
More protection for the butyl

Step-by-step: **Making the classic round pond**

Digging
*Work slowly, so the sides
of the hole don't collapse*

Hole shape
*If the earth at
the sides
crumbles, make
the hole wider
at the top*

1 Mark out a circle 2.028 m in diameter (and a patio area if required), and dig out the earth to a depth of 988 mm. The soil may crumble a little at the edges, but this is not a problem as long as the hole is at least 2.028 m in diameter at the bottom. If the ground is hard and rocky, break it up with a pickaxe or mattock.

Top
*Use bricks to hold the
top of the textile in place*

Bottom
*Remove sharp
stones before
laying the
geo-textile*

Sides
*Be generous
and allow a
big overlap*

2 Remove sharp stones from the hole and line it with sand followed by geo-textile. Cover the bottom first and then drape it up the sides, with evenly distributed folds and overlaps of 100 mm or more at the joins. Make sure that it overlaps the top of the hole by at least 300 mm. Weigh down the edges with bricks.

Butyl
*Use bricks to hold the
top edge in place*

Sides
*Try to distribute
the folds
equally around
the sides*

3 Cover the geo-textile with a single sheet of butyl. (Don't put water in the hole to help spread it.) Keep rearranging it so that it takes up the shape of the pond and the folds are evenly distributed. It should overlap the edge of the pond by at least 300 mm; weigh down the top edge with bricks.

Geo-textile
*Cover the butyl with
geo-textile as in step 2*

Concrete
*Lay a 65 mm-
thick slab on
top of the
geo-textile*

Tamping
*Tamp the
concrete level
right up to
the sides of
the hole*

4 Spread a second layer of geo-textile over the butyl, overlap the edges and weigh it down. Ask a friend to help you lay a slab of 65 mm-thick concrete in the bottom of the pond, smoothing it out with a tamping beam (fix handles to the beam with nails) operated from ground level. Allow the concrete to dry for two days.

Horizontal level
Check the level of every course of bricks

Vertical level
Use the spirit level to ensure that the walls are vertical and true

5 Build a round brick wall, ten bricks high, on top of the concrete (diameter is approx. 1.635 m). You may prefer to use a trammel to establish the circle (see pages 27 and 100). Allow 10 mm-thick mortar joints, scrape away excess mortar and clean the joints before the mortar dries. Check vertical and horizontal levels during construction. Add an eleventh course, overlapping the previous one by about 15 mm, to give a decorative stepped edge to the pond (diameter is 1.605 m).

Trammel
Use a trammel to ensure that the edge forms a true circle

Patio
If you are going to surround the pond with a patio, dig out the earth around the pond. Spread 50 mm of hardcore, 30 mm of compacted ballast, and 13 mm of uncompacted sharp sand over the area

6 Fold the pond lining (geo-textile and butyl) over the wall and into the pond. Fill the cavity between the wall and the earth with sand. Trim the pond lining level with the bricks. Make a trammel (or if you used one in step 5, extend it) that indicates a circle 1.585 m in diameter, and lay the twelfth course of bricks around the edge of the pond. The trammel consists of a plywood base, placed on a workbench. The base holds the trammel support block, surrounded by bricks to keep it in place and weigh down the base. The trammel arm pivots on a nail in the trammel support block. A U-shaped trammel piece is fixed to the trammel arm to indicate the position of the edge bricks, which are laid to meet the end of the trammel at 90°. Finish work on the surrounding area.

Inspirations: Decorative brickwork

Bricks are inherently decorative in their own right, with a colour range that ascends from slate blue and black to red, encompassing a rainbow of oranges, yellows and umbers in between. The other beauty of bricks is that they can be laid in decorative patterns to make even the most pedestrian structure look exciting. Patterns can be formed according to an array of traditional bonds, or created by inserting bricks of various colours, or even made by including different materials such as tiles.

ABOVE A simple but very decorative garden wall, with three courses set in a honeycomb pattern under a coping of soldier bricks.

ABOVE (INSET) A traditional English Sussex farmyard wall with the bricks set in a heading bond (the courses run at a diagonal angle to the ground).

ABOVE Stark winter weather reveals the full decorative structure of these pergola pillars. It has been achieved by setting selected bricks slightly proud of the primary face, to create a subtle diaper pattern (see page 28), and also by topping the pillars with chevron or zigzag headers, formed by setting a course of bricks to show a series of faces at angles of 45° to the general surface of the pillar.

Brick barbecue

This impressive structure beats other barbecues hollow in terms of attractiveness and practicality. There is a huge area for cooking, large work surfaces, a couple of handy shelves, and a hearth chimney for the smoke. It makes an eye-catching garden feature, and out of barbecue season, the work surfaces and shelves would be good for displaying plants (place containers on saucers to avoid marking the surfaces).

TIME

Five days (assuming there is an existing foundation).

SAFETY

Do not leave a lit barbecue unattended, especially if you have young children and pets.

YOU WILL NEED

Materials *for a barbecue 1.606 m high, 1.565 m wide and 832 mm deep*
- Bricks: 377
- Concrete slabs: 4 slabs, 441 mm square and 30 mm thick
- Tiles: 30 tiles, 150 mm square and 8 mm thick
- Slate: 6 random, fairly oval pieces, about 50 mm in diameter and 8 mm thick
- Mortar: 1 part (40 kg) cement and 4 parts (160 kg) sand
- Wood: 9 pieces, 192 mm long, 35 mm wide and 22 mm thick (sticks for centre of former);
  1 piece, 460 mm long, 35 mm wide and 22 mm thick (trammel);
  1 piece, 1.7 m long, 35 mm wide and 20 mm thick (straight-edge)
- Plywood: 2 pieces, 720 mm long, 360 mm wide and 6 mm thick (former)
- Nails: 18 x 30 mm
- Grill kit: between 640–685 mm x 348–450 mm

Tools
- Tape measure, straight-edge and piece of chalk
- Spade, fork and shovel
- Wheelbarrow and bucket
- Sledgehammer
- Shovel and mixing board, or cement mixer
- Bricklayer's trowel and pointing trowel
- Mason's hammer and club hammer
- Bolster chisel
- Rubber mallet
- Spirit level
- General-purpose saw
- Jigsaw
- Claw hammer

EATING OUT

Everyone enjoys a barbecue – there is something very appealing about cooking and eating food outdoors in warm weather. This barbecue is ideal if you do a lot of entertaining, because it is bigger than average and built to last. It will banish forever those barbecuing balancing acts with tiny, feeble contraptions that seem to rust as you look at them.

Take considerable care when deciding on a location for the barbecue. It is obviously not feasible to move the completed structure, so before committing to a spot, have a trial cooking session there on a disposable barbecue. Watch out for hazards such as low branches, or plants growing on a pergola overhead that might shrivel in the heat or catch fire, and drawbacks such as being just too far away from the seating area. The barbecue needs a firm foundation, so check what is under your existing patio (see page 21) or build a new foundation as shown on page 110.

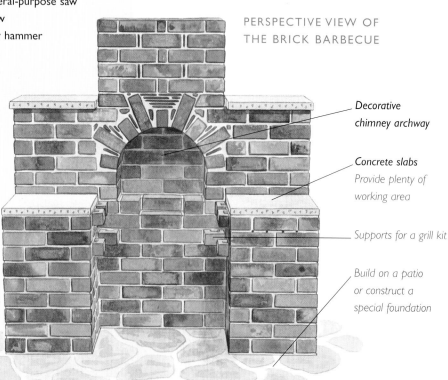

PERSPECTIVE VIEW OF THE BRICK BARBECUE

Decorative chimney archway

Concrete slabs
Provide plenty of working area

Supports for a grill kit

Build on a patio or construct a special foundation

Brick barbecue

PLAN VIEW SHOWING THE LAYOUT OF THE FIRST COURSE OF BRICKS

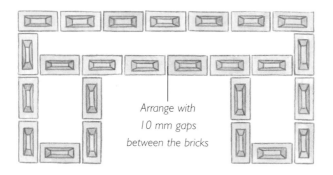

Arrange with 10 mm gaps between the bricks

PLAN VIEW SHOWING THE LAYOUT OF THE SECOND COURSE OF BRICKS

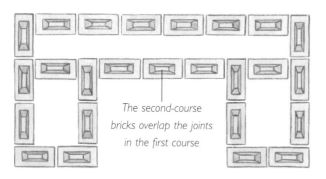

The second-course bricks overlap the joints in the first course

PLAN VIEW SHOWING THE LAYOUT OF THE SEVENTH COURSE OF BRICKS

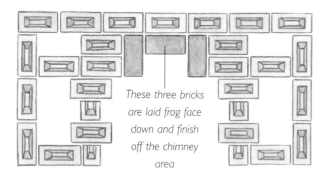

These three bricks are laid frog face down and finish off the chimney area

PLAN VIEW SHOWING THE LAYOUT OF THE NINTH COURSE OF BRICKS

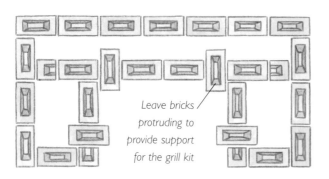

Leave bricks protruding to provide support for the grill kit

FRONT VIEW OF THE ARCH FORMER (ONE SIDE REMOVED)

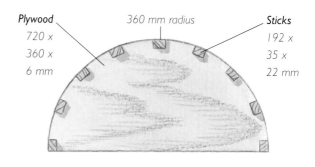

Plywood
720 x 360 x 6 mm

360 mm radius

Sticks
192 x 35 x 22 mm

PERSPECTIVE VIEW OF THE ARCH FORMER

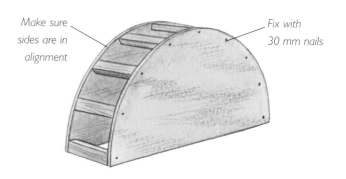

Make sure sides are in alignment

Fix with 30 mm nails

SIDE VIEW OF THE BRICK BARBECUE

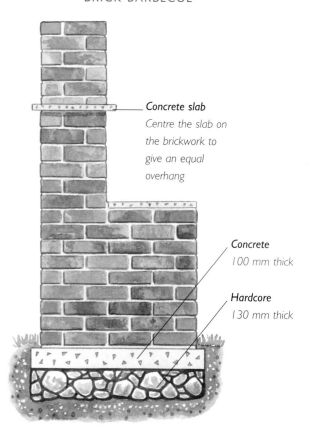

Concrete slab
Centre the slab on the brickwork to give an equal overhang

Concrete
100 mm thick

Hardcore
130 mm thick

EXPLODED VIEW OF
THE BRICK BARBECUE

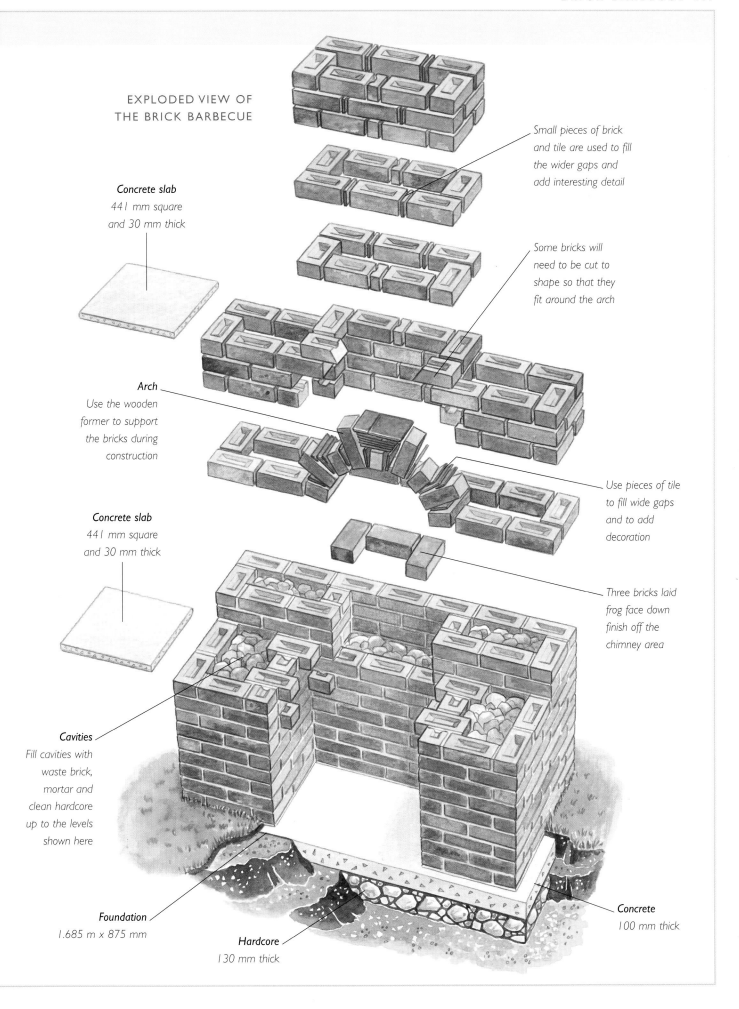

*Small pieces of brick
and tile are used to fill
the wider gaps and
add interesting detail*

Concrete slab
*441 mm square
and 30 mm thick*

*Some bricks will
need to be cut to
shape so that they
fit around the arch*

Arch
*Use the wooden
former to support
the bricks during
construction*

*Use pieces of tile
to fill wide gaps
and to add
decoration*

Concrete slab
*441 mm square
and 30 mm thick*

*Three bricks laid
frog face down
finish off the
chimney area*

Cavities
*Fill cavities with
waste brick,
mortar and
clean hardcore
up to the levels
shown here*

Foundation
1.685 m x 875 mm

Hardcore
130 mm thick

Concrete
100 mm thick

Step-by-step: **Making the brick barbecue**

First course
*Spend time perfecting
the layout*

Mortar
*Use a fairly stiff mortar
for the first course*

Guidelines
*Draw around
the layout
with chalk*

Squareness
*It is vital that
the angles
are at 90°*

Levelling
*Make
adjustments to
ensure that the
bricks are level*

1 If you do not have an existing patio area that provides a firm foundation on which to build, dig a 230 mm-deep hole and lay 130 mm of compacted hardcore and 100 mm of concrete (add 50 mm to the depth of the hole if the barbecue will be surrounded by grass – this allows the bricks to merge into the grass). Mark out the outer area of the barbecue and practise arranging your first course of bricks (without mortar) in the order shown. Check that the grill and tray fit.

2 If you are working on an existing patio, check that it is level in all directions before proceeding. If it does slope, it can probably be compensated for by adding extra mortar in the first course. If the slope is too great (more than 10 mm across the length of the barbecue), you will need to cast a level concrete slab on top, at least 40 mm thick. Begin laying the first course of bricks.

Corners
*As you build
the corners,
check that they
are true with
the spirit level*

Waste
*All the brick and mortar waste
can be put into the cavities*

Supports
*Centre the
support bricks
across the
thickness of
the wall*

Levels
*Ensure the
support bricks
are level with
each other*

3 Continue building up the walls, making sure all the joints are staggered and that the structure is level and vertical. Check each brick with the spirit level before proceeding to the next, and take time to finish off the joints between bricks before the mortar dries.

4 Complete six courses, and on the seventh course change the layout of bricks as shown, so that four bricks stick out into the recess. The ends of these bricks provide support for the metal tray.

Grill
The grill will finish up two
courses higher than the tray

Arch
Use mortar and slate to correct
the angle of bricks around the arch

Levels
Make
adjustments to
ensure the grill
and tray are
level and
parallel with
each other

Supports
Use thin bits
of wood or
slate to level
the former

Former
Propped up
on bricks

 5 Continue building upward and incorporate support for the grill in the ninth course. Check that both the tray and grill fit in the recess, and then put them aside. At this stage, the brickwork either side of the recess is complete and you can now concentrate on the back of the barbecue. Make a wooden former to support the brickwork arch as in the Tudor Arch Wall Niche project on pages 94–99.

6 Prop up the former on bricks. Build the arch over it, using pieces of slate to help prop up the bricks over the arch. Starting from one side, put mortar on the bricks that are already there, then place one of the arch bricks, making sure it is pointing to the centre of the arch (if not, push a piece of slate underneath to prop it to the correct angle). Continue laying bricks around the arch, and when you are almost at the centre, start at the other side. Finish by inserting a central brick.

Courses
Make sure the bricks are
level each side of the arch

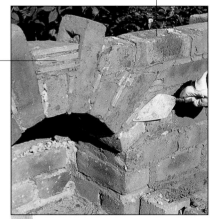

Tiles
Use broken
tiles to make
decorative infills

Levels
Make repeated
checks with the
spirit level

Worktops
Use mortar
and slate to
level the slabs

7 Fill the cavities in the barbecue, up to the the level of the grill, with waste brick, mortar and clean hardcore. Fill in the area over the arch with bricks cut to size and pieces of decorative tile. Use the pointing trowel to fill any gaps and tidy up the mortar joints as you build.

8 Complete building the chimney stack, checking levels as you work. Check the concrete slab surfaces fit and bed them level on a 10 mm-thick layer of mortar. Finish off all the mortar joints. Wait a few days before having a barbecue, or the heat will dry out the mortar too quickly.

Feature wall

An ancient brick wall is a unique piece of history, as well as a charming structure. It is a record of changing needs – as time passes, doors and windows are altered and filled in with bits of this and that. This project aims to achieve a similar patchwork of interesting features. If you wish, you can make it as a piece of art that reflects your own personal history, with structures and textures to represent significant events in your own life, such as marriage or the birth of a child.

<table>
<tr><td>TIME</td></tr>
<tr><td>Six days (do not lay more than four courses in a day).</td></tr>
<tr><td>SAFETY</td></tr>
<tr><td>Add a buttress behind the wall to make it safer if you have children (see page 29).</td></tr>
</table>

YOU WILL NEED

Materials *for a wall 1.714 m high and 2.578 m long*
- Bricks: 306
- Stone: 1 slab, 430 mm long, 240 mm wide and 60 mm thick; 2 boulders, 200 mm in diameter; 14 small pieces, 300 mm long, 200 mm wide and 30 mm thick
- Millstone: 410 mm in diameter and 110 mm thick
- Tiles: 9 tiles, 215 mm long, 162 mm wide and 10 mm thick
- Cobbles: 40 cobbles, 50 mm in diameter
- Pebbles: 150 pebbles, 15 mm in diameter
- Hardcore: 0.2 cu. metres
- Concrete: 1 part (60 kg) cement and 4 parts (240 kg) ballast
- Mortar: 1 part (60 kg) cement and 4 parts (240 kg) sand
- Wood: 8 pieces, 204 mm long, 35 mm wide and 22 mm thick (sticks for centre of former); 1 piece, 560 mm long, 35 mm wide and 22 mm thick (trammel)
- Plywood: 2 pieces, 460 mm long, 395 mm wide and 6 mm thick (former)
- Nails: 16 x 40 mm

Tools
- Tape measure, pegs, string, straight-edge and a piece of chalk
- Spade and fork
- Wheelbarrow and bucket
- Sledgehammer
- Shovel and mixing board, or cement mixer
- Bricklayer's trowel and pointing trowel
- Mason's hammer and club hammer
- Bolster chisel
- Spirit level
- General-purpose saw
- Jigsaw
- Claw hammer

PLAN VIEW SHOWING THE
FIRST COURSE OF BRICKS

*Foundation
2.650 m x 300 mm*

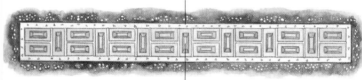

*Two-brick-thick wall
Laid in a Flemish bond*

PLAN VIEW SHOWING THE
SECOND COURSE OF BRICKS

*In the second course, the bricks are laid so
that they overlap the joints in the first course*

TIME AND TEXTURE

There is something fascinating about walking through the ruins of a once-magnificent castle or abbey, and seeing crumbling archways held up as if by magic, and staircases that lead nowhere. Wouldn't it be great to have your own mysterious ruin at the bottom of the garden? Well, now is your chance to build something unusual with a historical feel.

This wall is 1.714 m high, and so needs a strong foundation as illustrated on page 116. We haven't built reinforcing piers or buttresses, because the wall is at the bottom of the garden beside a hedge and is unlikely to be disturbed, but if you have children who are likely to play nearby, you must include extra support (see Supporting Piers and Buttresses on page 29).

All sorts of brick and stone materials can be built into this wall, so don't feel that you have to follow the drawings exactly. Pieces of carved stone, fossils or even shells would also look great bedded in the mortar.

Feature wall

FRONT VIEW OF
THE ARCH FORMER
(ONE SIDE REMOVED)

PERSPECTIVE VIEW OF
THE ARCH FORMER

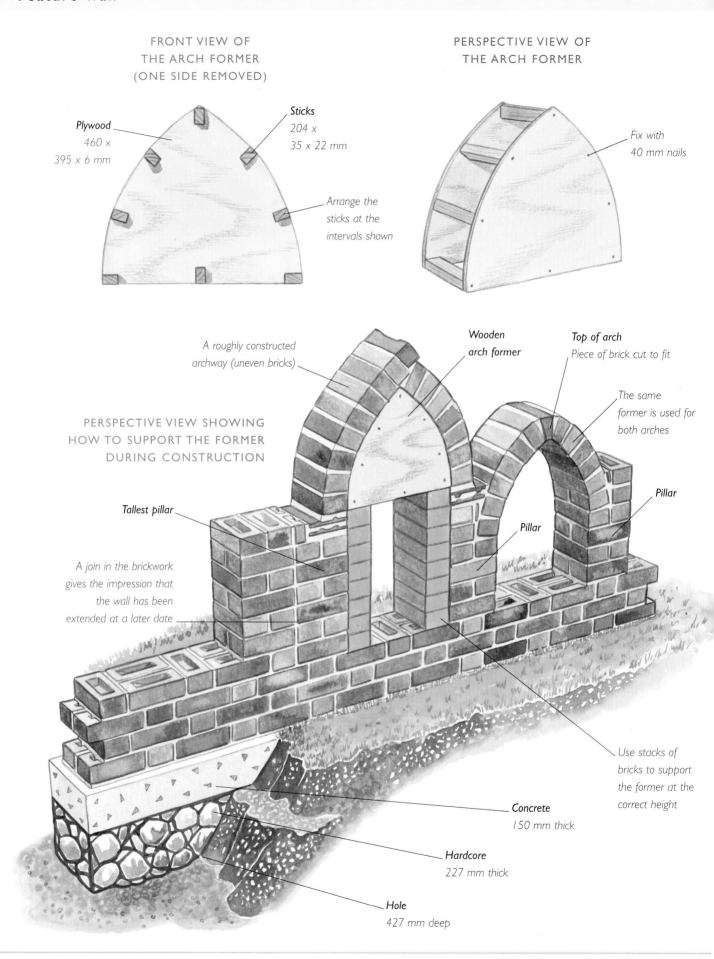

Plywood
460 x
395 x 6 mm

Sticks
204 x
35 x 22 mm

*Arrange the
sticks at the
intervals shown*

*Fix with
40 mm nails*

*A roughly constructed
archway (uneven bricks)*

*Wooden
arch former*

Top of arch
Piece of brick cut to fit

*The same
former is used for
both arches*

PERSPECTIVE VIEW SHOWING
HOW TO SUPPORT THE FORMER
DURING CONSTRUCTION

Tallest pillar

*A join in the brickwork
gives the impression that
the wall has been
extended at a later date*

Pillar

Pillar

*Use stacks of
bricks to support
the former at the
correct height*

Concrete
150 mm thick

Hardcore
227 mm thick

Hole
427 mm deep

EXPLODED VIEW OF THE FEATURE WALL

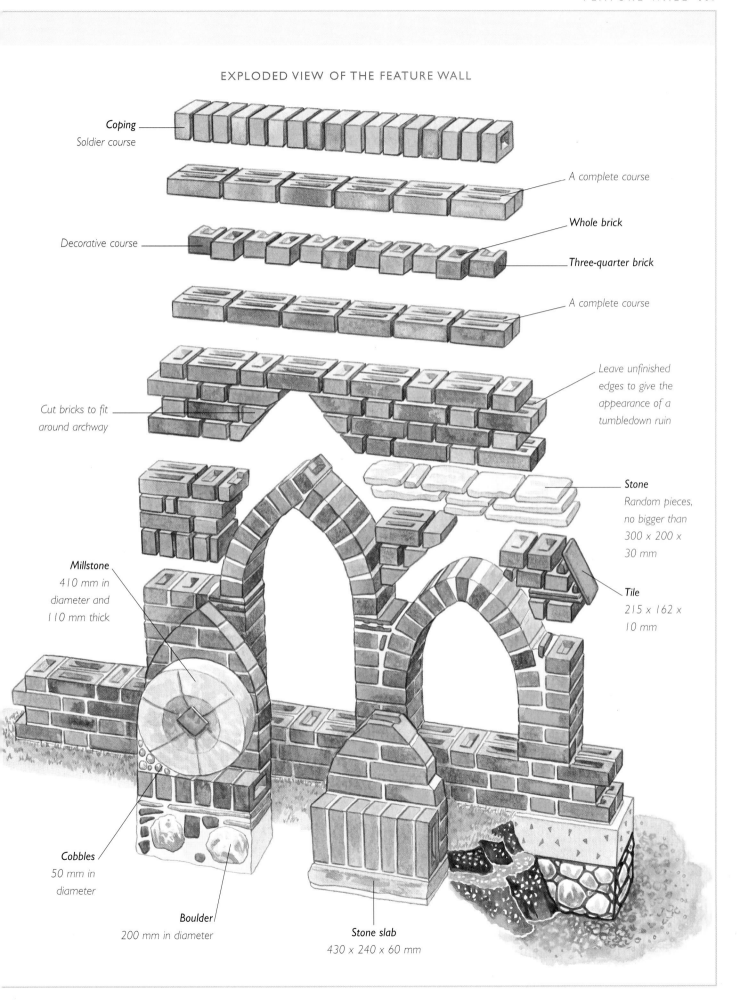

Coping
Soldier course

A complete course

Whole brick

Decorative course

Three-quarter brick

A complete course

Cut bricks to fit
around archway

Leave unfinished
edges to give the
appearance of a
tumbledown ruin

Stone
Random pieces,
no bigger than
300 x 200 x
30 mm

Millstone
410 mm in
diameter and
110 mm thick

Tile
215 x 162 x
10 mm

Cobbles
50 mm in
diameter

Boulder
200 mm in diameter

Stone slab
430 x 240 x 60 mm

Step-by-step: **Making the feature wall**

Bond
Use a Flemish bond to build
the wall three courses high

Spirit level
Ensure the pillars are
upright and parallel

Levels
Ensure the
pillars are level
with each other

Levels
Use the spirit
level to check
the levels

Pillar
Build two,
two-by-two
brick pillars

1 Dig a foundation hole 427 mm deep, and lay 227 mm of compacted hardcore and 150 mm of concrete. Use chalk and a string line or straight-edge to mark the position of the wall. Build three courses of bricks in the decorative bond shown. Make sure all the vertical joints are staggered and check that the wall is level and vertical. The finished wall is meant to look like an old structure that has been repaired many times over the years, so just finish the joints by scraping out excess mortar and don't bother filling gaps.

2 Build up two brick pillars (as shown here) and a third, taller pillar (as shown in the drawings on pages 116–117). Make sure all the bricks are turned so that they overlap the joints of the bricks below and check that they are level using the spirit level.

Top of arch
Use a piece of
brick cut to fit

Former
Refer to the
working
drawings for
the shape of
the former

Soldier bricks
Lay bricks on
their stretcher
face over
the former

Former
Propped up
on bricks

3 Make a wooden former to support the brickwork arch. You can draw the shape of the arch on the plywood using a trammel (see page 27) to make the two 460 mm-radius arcs. Cut out the arch shape with the jigsaw. Join the pieces together as shown in the Tudor Arch Wall Niche project on pages 94–99.

4 Prop up the wooden former on piles of bricks between the two small pillars. Lay bricks up each side of the arch, leaving equal spaces between each brick and tapping them down with the handle of the mason's hammer. At the top of the arch, lay a brick that has been cut to fit.

Stepped detail
Use tiles to build
idiosyncratic details

Top of arch
Bricks cut to fit

Bond
Continue the
Flemish bond
over the arch

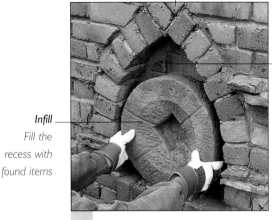

Detailing
Complete the
recess by filling
in around the
millstone with
mortar and
cobbles

Infill
Fill the
recess with
found items

5 Build around the arch with brick and pieces of tile and stone as shown in the drawing (or according to your own design). This is a good way of using up spare bricks and stone. When the mortar has dried, remove the wooden former and reuse it to build the second (higher) arch. Fill in the lower arch with bricks and stone. Brick up the back of the higher arch, using a single thickness of bricks.

6 Mortar the millstone in the recess of the higher arch and fill in around it with cobbles and mortar. Interesting salvaged architectural features or broken pieces of crockery could also be incorporated into the structure.

Soldier bricks
Top the wall
with a coping
of soldier bricks

7 Finish building the regular courses above the level of the arches and start on the decorative strips of bricks at the top. Cut bricks in half and use these for the recessed details. Complete the building process with a course of soldier bricks to form the coping.

Helpful hint

You can make brickwork look old and weathered by scraping mortar from between the bricks, and then using a wire brush to erode the mortar before it dries completely.

Waterspout

A small courtyard or a quiet corner of the garden can be magically enhanced by the addition of a waterspout. A gentle stream of water spouts through a mask, set into a brick wall topped by an arch, and splashes on to a couple of splash tiles protruding from the wall before tumbling into a reservoir pool. If you enjoy the therapeutic sight and sound of falling water, this striking project will make an exciting feature.

TIME

Five days (add a day if you need to build a foundation).

SAFETY

Do not leave small children unattended if there is a water feature in the garden.

YOU WILL NEED

Materials *for a wall, waterspout and reservoir 1.47 m high, 948 mm wide and 805 mm deep*
- Bricks: 205
- Tiles: 24 tiles, 245 mm long, 152 mm wide and 10 mm thick
- Mortar: 1 part (25 kg) cement and 4 parts (100 kg) sand
- Render: 1 part (25 kg) cement and 4 parts (100 kg) sharp sand
- Wood: 10 pieces, 193 mm long, 35 mm wide and 22 mm thick (sticks for centre of former); 1 piece, 446 mm long, 35 mm wide and 22 mm thick (trammel)
- Plywood: 2 pieces, 690 mm long, 345 mm wide and 6 mm thick (former)
- Nails: 20 x 40 mm
- Armoured plastic pipe: 4 m x 50 mm in diameter (to protect electric cable and water delivery pipe)
- Flexible plastic pipe (water delivery pipe): 2 m (to fit on pump and run through armoured pipe 50 mm in diameter)
- Small submersible pump
- Mask: 215–290 mm high
- Tanking paint: 1 litre

Tools
- Tape measure, straight-edge and piece of chalk
- Hacksaw to cut pipe
- Wheelbarrow and bucket
- Shovel and mixing board, or cement mixer
- Bricklayer's trowel and pointing trowel
- Mason's hammer and club hammer
- Bolster chisel
- Spirit level
- General-purpose saw
- Jigsaw
- Claw hammer

WATER SETS THE MOOD

Fountains, waterfalls, cascades and waterspouts all make great garden or courtyard features – the sight and sound of water trickling or splashing into a pool below is mesmerising and relaxing. The waterspout is a fairly traditional feature in formal, classical gardens, but is also perfect for modern gardens of all descriptions.

This design has the advantage of being freestanding, but most waterspout designs rely on fixing a mask to an existing wall, which entails installing pipework within the wall for the water and power supplies, and this is quite an engineering job. With this project, you don't need an existing wall (but you can build it in front of a wall) and the pipework is concealed within a cavity at the back of the structure.

You may like to consider variations in the overall shape of the structure (perhaps smaller, or squared off at the top), or add decoration such as ornate tile details. You may prefer a different type of wall mask: we have chosen a strong character, but you could have something more restrained like a lion's head, or even design and make something of your own in clay or copper.

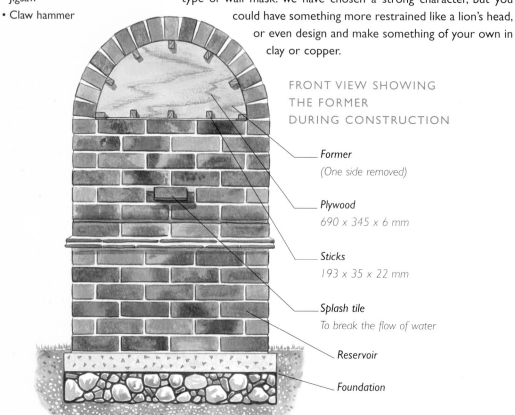

FRONT VIEW SHOWING
THE FORMER
DURING CONSTRUCTION

Former
(One side removed)

Plywood
690 x 345 x 6 mm

Sticks
193 x 35 x 22 mm

Splash tile
To break the flow of water

Reservoir

Foundation

Waterspout

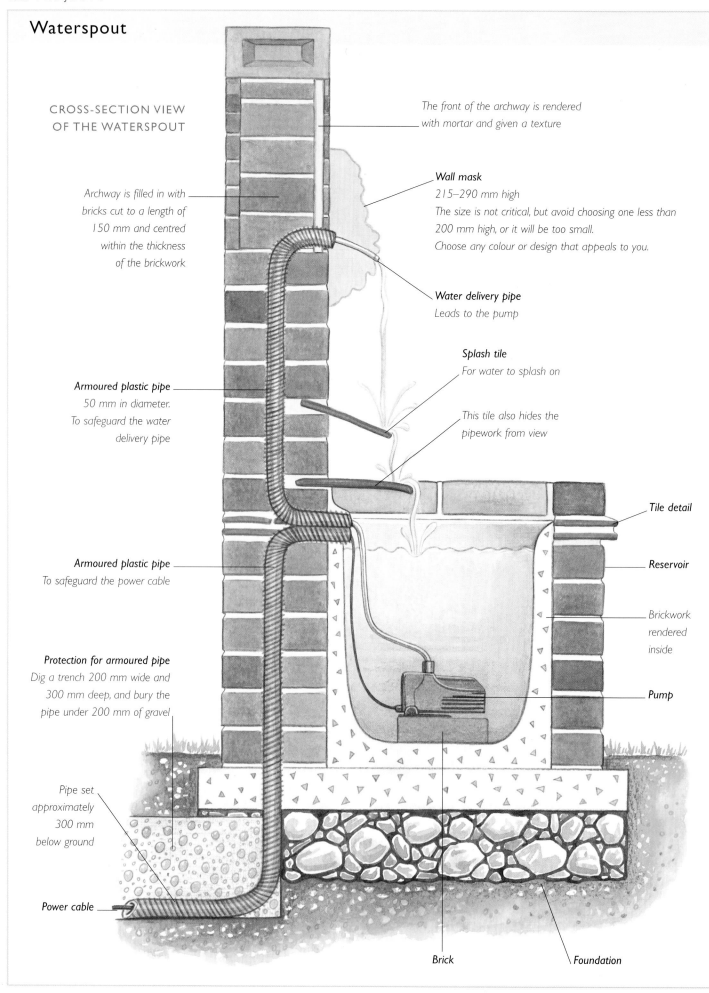

CROSS-SECTION VIEW
OF THE WATERSPOUT

The front of the archway is rendered
with mortar and given a texture

Archway is filled in with
bricks cut to a length of
150 mm and centred
within the thickness
of the brickwork

Wall mask
215–290 mm high
The size is not critical, but avoid choosing one less than
200 mm high, or it will be too small.
Choose any colour or design that appeals to you.

Water delivery pipe
Leads to the pump

Splash tile
For water to splash on

Armoured plastic pipe
50 mm in diameter.
To safeguard the water
delivery pipe

This tile also hides the
pipework from view

Tile detail

Armoured plastic pipe
To safeguard the power cable

Reservoir

Brickwork
rendered
inside

Protection for armoured pipe
Dig a trench 200 mm wide and
300 mm deep, and bury the
pipe under 200 mm of gravel

Pump

Pipe set
approximately
300 mm
below ground

Power cable

Brick

Foundation

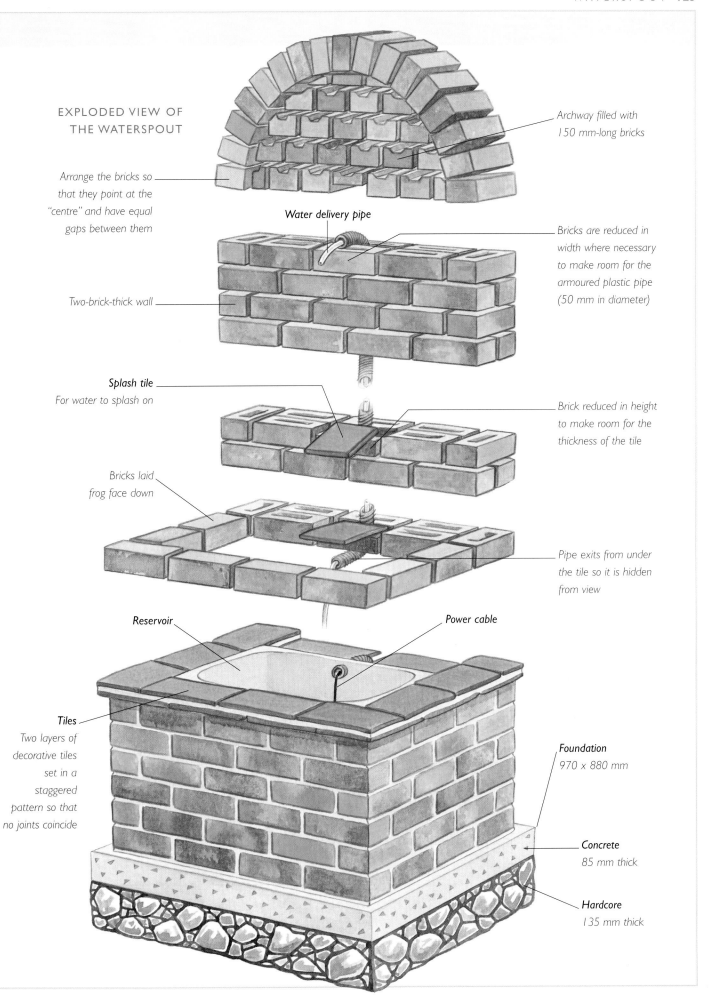

EXPLODED VIEW OF
THE WATERSPOUT

*Arrange the bricks so
that they point at the
"centre" and have equal
gaps between them*

*Archway filled with
150 mm-long bricks*

Water delivery pipe

*Bricks are reduced in
width where necessary
to make room for the
armoured plastic pipe
(50 mm in diameter)*

Two-brick-thick wall

Splash tile
For water to splash on

*Brick reduced in height
to make room for the
thickness of the tile*

*Bricks laid
frog face down*

*Pipe exits from under
the tile so it is hidden
from view*

Reservoir

Power cable

Tiles
*Two layers of
decorative tiles
set in a
staggered
pattern so that
no joints coincide*

Foundation
970 x 880 mm

Concrete
85 mm thick

Hardcore
135 mm thick

Step-by-step: Making the waterspout

Back wall
Incorporate a second wall at the back of the box

Pipes
Build in two armoured pipes – one for water and one for power

Bond
Build the wall using a stretcher bond

Courses
After every few courses, scrape off excess mortar and tidy up the joints between the bricks

Coping tiles
Top the wall with a double-tile coping

1 Find a firm area of patio to build on (with a suitable foundation – see page 21), or construct a level foundation using 135 mm of compacted hardcore and 85 mm of concrete. Mark out the area of the brickwork. Build the reservoir: a simple box shape that incorporates a second wall at the back for housing the pipes. Cut bricks to fit around the armoured pipe containing the electric cable.

2 Continue building until you have completed six courses. Lay two courses of tiles on 10 mm-thick mortar. Overlap the joints as shown, and avoid cutting them if possible. If the tiles are curved, lay them so the bottom layer curves upward and the top layer curves downward. Position the armoured pipe for the water delivery pipe.

Splash tile
The distance the tiles protrude, and their angle, affect the way the water falls. Experiment with tiles propped up in position under the mask before starting construction. Pour water through the mask to ascertain how the tiles should be placed for best effect. Take measurements from this mock-up

3 To top the reservoir, lay a line of bricks (frog side down) around the box shape. Finish the joint between the bricks and the tiles with an angled mortar detail. Fix a splash tile into the back wall. Continue building the back wall, cutting bricks where necessary to fit around the water delivery pipe. Refer to the drawings to see how the bricks are laid for best effect.

Helpful hint

Some of the bricks around the pipe require cutting lengthwise, but for the rest it is enough just to break off the corner with a hammer.

Former
Plywood or other
waste wood

Arch
Run bricks around the arch, laying
them on their stretcher face

Trammel
Use the
trammel to
draw semicircles
with a radius
of 345 mm

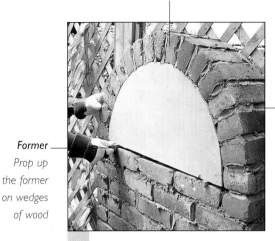

Arch bricks
Use a bit of
waste tile to
space the
arch bricks

Former
Prop up
the former
on wedges
of wood

4 Complete building the back wall, incorporating a second splash tile and finishing with the water delivery pipe sticking out of the centre of the cavity. Make a wooden former for the arch shape: mark semicircles with a 345 mm radius on the plywood using a trammel (see page 27). Cut out with the jigsaw. Join the pieces together as described in the Tudor Arch Wall Niche project on pages 94–99.

5 Place the former on small scraps of wood and practise placing bricks (on their stretcher face) around the curve. When you are confident and ready to start, lay each brick on a generous angled bed of mortar, and tap it down into position. If you need to make major corrections, it is better to start again with fresh mortar. Remove the former by pulling out the scraps of wood beneath.

6 Brick up the back of the wall under the arch with bricks that have been reduced in length and laid with the header faces (ends) facing forwards. Leave the water delivery pipe poking out at the front, level with the bottom of the arch. Render the arch recess and texture it with a piece of wood. Render the inside of the reservoir pool with mortar made with sharp sand, allow to dry and coat with tanking paint. After a few days, fit the mask and install the pump.

Pipe
As you render
around the
pipe, make
sure that it
doesn't slip
back into
the wall

Rendering
Cover the recessed
arch with mortar
and create a
grooved texture
with a piece of
waste wood

Glossary

Backfilling To fill or pack a cavity (behind a wall or in a foundation trench hole) with earth in order to bring the ground up to the desired level.

Bedding The process of pressing a brick, slab or stone into a bed or layer of wet mortar and ensuring that it is level.

Buttering The act of using a trowel during bricklaying to cover some part of a brick with wet mortar, prior to setting it in position on a bed of mortar.

Compacting Using a sledgehammer or the weight of the body to press down a layer of sand, earth or hardcore.

Coursing Part of the process of bricklaying – bedding a number of bricks on a bed of mortar in order to build a course (a horizontal layer of bricks).

Curing time The time taken for mortar or concrete to become firm and stable. "Part-cured" means that the mortar or concrete is firm enough to bear a small amount of weight.

Floating The procedure of using a metal, plastic or wooden float to skim wet concrete or mortar to a smooth and level finish.

Levelling Using a spirit level to decide whether or not a structure or brick is level (horizontally parallel to the ground, or vertically at right angles to the ground), and then making adjustments to bring individual bricks into line.

Marking out Using string, pegs and a tape measure to variously set out the area of a foundation on the ground. Also to mark an individual brick in readiness for cutting.

Pecking Using the edge of a large trowel or the chisel end of a mason's hammer to nibble the ragged edge of a part-cut brick back to a marked line.

Planning The procedure of considering a project, viewing the site, making drawings, working out quantities and costs, prior to starting work. Thorough planning is vital in order to avoid hold-ups and the wastage of materials.

Pointing Using a trowel, stick or a tool of your choice to bring mortar joints to the desired finish.

Raking out Using a trowel to rake out some part of the mortar from between courses, so that the edges of the bricks are clearly and crisply revealed.

Sighting To judge by eye whether or not a cut, joint or structure is level or true. To look down or along a wall in order to determine whether or not the structure is level.

Siting Deciding whereabouts on the site – in the garden or on the plot – the structure is going to be placed. The aspect, sun, shade and proximity to the house may need to be taken into consideration.

Sourcing Questioning suppliers by phone, e-mail or letter, in order to make decisions concerning the best source for materials – especially sand, cement and bricks.

Tamping The act of using a length of wood to compact and level wet concrete.

Trial run or dry run Setting out the components of a structure, without using concrete or mortar, in order to ascertain whether or not the pattern of bricks is going to work out.

Trimming Using a hammer or the edge of a large trowel to cut and sculpt a brick to a good finish.

Watering Wetting bricks at the start of a work session, prior to bedding them on mortar.

Wire brushing Using a wire-bristled brush to remove dry mortar from the face of bricks, for example on a wall, or the surface of a path or patio.

Suppliers

UK

Bricks, concrete, cement

Baggeridge Brick Plc
Fir Street
Sedgley
Dudley
West Midlands
DY3 4AA
Tel: (01902) 880555
Fax: (01902) 880432
www.baggeridge.co.uk
(Suppliers of bricks, pavers etc.)

Freshfield Lane Brickworks
Dane Hill
Haywards Heath
West Sussex
RH17 7HH
Tel: (01825) 790350
www.flb.uk.com

Heritage Reclaimed Brick Co.
Unit 2, 24 Willow Lane
Mitcham
Surrey
CR4 4NA
Tel: (020) 8687 1907

Ibstock Bricks Ltd
Ashdown Works
Turkey Road
Bexhill-on-Sea
East Sussex
TN39 5HY
Tel: (01424) 847400

The Brick Warehouse
18–22 Northdown Street
London
N1 9BG
Tel: (020) 7833 9992

York Handmade Brick
   Company Ltd
Winchester House
Forest Lane
Alne
York
YO61 1TU
Tel: (01347) 838881
Fax: (01347) 838885
www.yorkhandmade.co.uk
(Suppliers of handmade bricks, paving materials and special shapes)

**General DIY Outlets
(branches nationwide)**

B & Q Plc
1 Hampshire Corporate Park
Chandlers Ford
Eastleigh
Hampshire
SO53 3YX
Tel: (01703) 256256

Focus Do-It-All Group Ltd
Gawsworth House
Westmere Drive
Crewe
Cheshire
CW1 6XB
Tel: (01384) 456456

Homebase Ltd
Beddington House
Railway Approach
Wallington
Surrey
SM6 0HB
Tel: (020) 8784 7200

Wickes
Wickes House
120–138 Station Road
Harrow
Middlesex
HA1 2QB
Tel: (0870) 6089001

SOUTH AFRICA

Bricks, concrete, cement

Cement and Concrete Institute
Portland Park
Old Pretoria Road
Halfway House
Midrand 1685
Tel: (011) 315 0300

Clay Brick Association
PO Box 1284
Halfway House
Johannesburg 1685
Tel: (011) 805 4206

Natal Master Builders'
Association Centre
40 Essex Terrace
Westville 3630
Tel: (031) 266 7070

The Building Centre
Belmont Square
Rondebosch
Cape Town 7700
Tel: (021) 685 3040

AUSTRALIA

ABC Timber & Building Supplies
46 Auburn Road
Regents Park
NSW 2143
Tel: (02) 9645 2511

BBC Hardware
Bld A
Cnr. Cambridge &
    Chester Streets
Epping
NSW 2121
Tel: (02) 9876 0888

Bowens Timber &
    Building Supplies
135–173 Macaulay Road
North Melbourne
VIC 3051
Tel: (03) 9328 1041

Bunnings Building Supplies
152 Pilbara Street
Welshpool
WA 6106
Tel: (08) 9365 1555

Elite Paving
33 Neilson Crescent
Bligh Park
NSW 2756
Tel: (4574 1414)

Pine Rivers Landscaping Supplies
93 South Pine Road
Strathpine
QLD 4500
Tel: (07) 3205 6708

Sydney Stone Yard
1/3A Stanley Road
Randwick
NSW 2031
Tel: (02) 9326 4479

NEW ZEALAND

Firth Industries
Freephone: 0800 800 576

Placemakers
Freephone: 0800 425 2269

Stevenson Building Supplies
Freephone: 0800 610 710
(Blocks, bricks, paving, concrete)

Southtile
654 North Road
Invercargill
Tel: (03) 215 9179
Freephone: 0800 768 848
(Tiles and bricks)

ITM Building Centres
Freephone: 0800 367 486

Conversion chart

To convert the metric measurements used in this book to imperial measurements, simply multiply the figure given in the text by the relevant number in the table alongside. Bear in mind that conversions will not necessarily work out exactly, and you will need to round the figure up or down slightly. (Do not use a combination of metric and imperial measurements – for accuracy, keep to one system.)

To convert	Multiply by
millimetres to inches	0.0394
metres to feet	3.28
metres to yards	1.093
sq. millimetres to sq. inches	0.00155
sq. metres to sq. feet	10.76
sq. metres to sq. yards	1.195
cu. metres to cu. feet	35.31
cu. metres to cu. yards	1.308
grams to pounds	0.0022
kilograms to pounds	2.2046
litres to gallons	0.22

Index